Rob's Recollections

of the Early History of
Whitewater Township
and
Skegemog Point
Grand Traverse County, Michigan

by
Robert Lucius Samels

Limited Edition

Number _427_

Cover sketch of Robert and Ben Samels

    by Glen McCune of McCune & Company of East Jordan, Michigan,

    based on a photo by Randy McCune of Natural Expressions of Petoskey, Michigan.

Cover design by Jennifer Watson

Edited by Claude M. Watson

Published by Meacham Publishing

Printed by Thomson-Shore, Dexter, Michigan

ISBN 0-9713335-0-5

Copyright © 2001 by
Robert Lucius Samels

Dedication

I dedicate this history to my parents Frank and Mary (Laubscher) Samels and my three brothers; Amos Lynn Samels, Frank Dennis Samels, Ben Wilbur Samels.

Mary Laubscher came with her brother Ben in 1883 from Meinsberg, Switzerland. They came all alone to Elk Rapids to be with their father who came a few years earlier. Mary was eleven years old and her brother was thirteen when they came, their mother having died in Switzerland when Mary was four years old and Ben was six years old. In 1892 Mary Laubscher married Frank Samels, who was the son of William and Miriam (Watson) Samels. Frank was born near what was later called Mabel, Whitewater Township, Grand Traverse County, Michigan.

I have written this from memory of what I remember since I was six or seven years old and what my father and mother told me of what happened before that.

Robert Lucius Samels

Acknowledgements

The editor and author are indebted for the help they have received. While it is not possible to name everyone, special thanks go to the following:

Betty and Kim Acker	Williamsburg Historians
Karon Anderson	Photo Collection
Kathi Waggoner Gober	Postcard Collection
Carl Goss	Photo Collection
Brenda Moore	Grand Traverse Genealogist
Glenn Neumann	Elk Rapids Area Historical Society
Linda Peckham	Lansing Comunity College
Clint and Doris Stites	
Doris Waggoner	Hotel Register
Gloria Wiltzer	Photo

Steve Harold, Grand Traverse Pioneer and Historical Society

Hardware and software used by the editor and publisher, Claude M. Watson:

Equipment:

Computer	Dell Dimension
Printer	HP DeskJet 1600CM
Scanner	UMAX Astra 1200S

Software:

Operating System	Microsoft Windows 98
Genealogy	Brothers Keeper V6
Typesetting	PC TeX/LaTeX V4
CAD program	Bentley MicroStation 95
Photo Editor	Paint Shop Pro 7

Contents

PART 1 History of Whitewater Township

Recollections 3
Whitewater Township 7
First Post Office for Whitewater Township 9
Gristmills and Sawmills in Whitewater 11
Business and Farming in Whitewater 17
Railroads 27
Lumbering in Whitewater 31
    Logging Camps 31
    Island Lake Camp 31
    Lumber Camps of Whitewater 33
    Square Timber Camp 35
Log Houses 37
Hunting and Fishing 39
People of Whitewater Township 41
    Early Settlers of Whitewater 41
    The First Generation in Whitewater Township 44
    People of Mabel, Whitewater Township 100 years ago .. 47
    The Silvers Family 53
    Entertainment 53
The Women of Whitewater Township 55
Doctors of Williamsburg 57
    Diphtheria 58
Cemeteries 59
Williamsburg 63
    Old Williamsburg 63
    New Town 67
Schools 69
Road Building and Maintenance in Whitewater Township 71
Garages of Williamsburg 73
Township Officers 75
Mabel 77
Baggs Road 79
Barker Creek 85
Old Settlers of Barker Creek 87
France or French Landing 89

Ice Storm 91
Boats and Railroads 93

PART 2 History of Skegemog Point
The Meaning of Skegemog 101
Indian History 103
Skegemog Point 105
Lumbering 109
People of Skegemog Point 111
    The First Settler 111
    Watson and Samels: Pioneer Families of Whitewater . 113
    Early Settlers 115
    People Born and Raised on Skegemog Road 118
Kings Hotel on the Point 121
    Caretakers at the Hotel 127
Boats on the Chain of Lakes: 129
Roads of Skegemog Point 131
    The First Automobile 135
Schools of Skegemog Road 137
Teachers of North Mabel School 138
Mabel 139
The Beauty Spot 141

Bibliography 143

List of Figures

1.1	1873 Elk Rapids newspaper advertisement	5
1.2	1881 Land Map of Whitewater Township	6
1.3	1905 Tourist Map	8
1.4	Gristmill Pond at Williamsburg about 1910	10
1.5	Trout Hatchery at Mill Pond	10
1.6	Kossuth Stites Sharpening Mill Saw Blade	12
1.7	Williamsburg Mill	15
1.8	Mill Race at Williamsburg	15
1.9	Pioneer Farm	16
1.10	Haywagon	16
1.11	Austin Pray plowing with Ed Pray's team	18
1.12	Bernie Scofield and Sylvia with team	18
1.13	Threshing at Orin Lindsey's, Mabel	20
1.14	Potato Loading	22
1.15	1896 Elk Rapids newspaper advertisement	24
1.16	James Watson packing apples	25
1.17	Train at Bates Station	26
1.18	Train at Williamsburg Station	26
1.19	1903 Island Lake Lumber Camp Crew with Big Wheels	30
1.20	Island Lake Lumber Camp, 1903	32
1.21	Log House	36
1.22	House Roofing Bee at Mabel, 1910	36
1.23	Dennis Samels, Fisherman	38
1.24	1900 Land Map of Whitewater Township	40
1.25	Benny Watson's 73rd Birthday, May 31, 1903	48
1.26	Weston and Sarah Jane Worden, 1908	51
1.27	Elk Rapids Progess Advertisments, December 1888	52
1.28	Sarah Lamson Watson beside her cabin	54
1.29	Dr. William Holdsworth's Office, Williamsburg	56
1.30	Elk Rapids Progress advertisement, 1896	58
1.31	Old Williamsburg Cemetery	60
1.32	Circle Hill Cemetery, Williamsburg	61
1.33	Williamsburg	62

1.34	View of Williamsburg	62
1.35	Hugo Wills Store (originally Vinton's, second Ennest's)	64
1.36	White's Store at Church and Vinton	65
1.37	Charles Wills' Hardware Store, 1908	66
1.38	Stores in New Town, c. 1921	66
1.39	Drake's Garage, Williamsburg	72
1.40	1882 Elk Rapids newspaper advertisement	74
1.41	1910 Mabel Train Wreck	78
1.42	1888 and 1895 Boat Schedules	84
1.43	Barker Creek Lumber Camp	87
1.44	Winter Snows	90
1.45	Winter at the Farm	90
1.46	Tugs Towing Cordwood	92
1.47	Fast Mail Train at Mabel	97
1.48	Michigan Railroads, 1897	98
2.49	1908 Map of Skegemog Point	102
2.50	Map of Skegemog Point, c. 1926	106
2.51	Ring and Spike	107
2.52	Map of Skegemog Point Settlers	110
2.53	Pioneers Frank and Mary Samels	112
2.54	Hotel Dock and Boathouse	120
2.55	Map of the Tip of Skegemog Point	120
2.56	King's Hotel	122
2.57	King's Hotel Staff	122
2.58	Diagram of King's Hotel	123
2.59	Hotel Register, 1928	125
2.60	Hotel Register, 1933	126
2.61	Steamer Ruth at Skegemog Point	128
2.62	The Mabel	128
2.63	South Mabel School Students, 1914	134
2.64	Rose and Ed Glendenning's First Auto	135
2.65	North Mabel School	136
2.66	North Mabel School Class, 1922	136
2.67	Mabel Church Group	139
2.68	Flowing Well at Mabel, 1908	140
2.69	Beauty Spot	141
2.70	Skegemog Point Road, 1908	142

Part I

History of Whitewater Township

Recollections

When our grandparents came in the 1850's, Whitewater Township was a wilderness covered with huge pine and hemlock. Many white pine were three and four feet through and some even five feet. There were also beech, maple, elm, oak and birch with a few basswood, also cedar and tamarack in the swamps.

Life was rugged. There were no roads. There were not more than one or two settlers, if any, east of what was later Williamsburg, and not more than three or four settlers in the township. The township was not organized yet. Supplies had to be brought up from Elk Rapids by boat or carried on foot. The boats were either sailboats or else rowboats, which had to be rowed by hand on Elk and Round Lake.

They had no crosscut saws. They had to chop their wood with an axe. They would chop a notch in a log and then split off sticks for firewood. Their only light was by tallow candle. They would fat up a cow or beef in the fall to get the tallow and make candles to last the year. One candle lasted two nights. Some settlers had candle molds that would make either six or 12 candles at once. They would loan these among their neighbors. Along in the 1870's Miriam Samels bought the first kerosene lamp. It consisted of a bowl which set in a base. It was two separate pieces together with a gallon of kerosene. Kerosene was a lot more powerful in those days. They were afraid of it. Her brother, Benny Watson, would come over to read by it as it gave a much brighter light than the candles. As soon as he was through reading, the lamp was put out and the candle was lit.

There were no railroads for almost 40 years after the first settlers came in. All supplies had to be brought into Elk Rapids or Traverse City by boat. In the fall enough supplies had to be brought in to last all winter 'til navigation opened up in the spring.

One fall the navigation closed before the last boat got in and left the country short of provisions before spring. Henry and Ed Noble ran the store in Elk Rapids. They rationed the provisions to the people, 15 lbs. of pork and so much flour to the family, and brought the settlers through the winter. There were some Indians at a lake out east who Nobles did not know about who starved to death. They called it Starvation Lake after that. The first boat in the spring brought in cornmeal. Everybody rushed to Elk Rapids to get cornmeal.

There were many Indians here then. When our grandparents came down here from Bruce Mines, Ontario, Canada, they brought a woman of French and Indian descent who could talk the Indian dialect and also English with them. The Indians would stop at our grandparents house to talk with her. She would then translate it into English to our grandparents. One morning they stopped and wanted to cook their breakfast on grandmother's stove. She let them and offered them the table to eat on, but they pushed it back and sat on the floor to eat their breakfast.

They learned from them (the Indians) that they held their camp meetings on Skegemog Point on the Round Lake side. When father was small in the 1870's, he saw more Indians than white people. He saw them on a march on what is now M-72, a string a mile long single file, each Indian about eight feet behind the other. The squaws had shawls the Government had given them tied full of stuff and carried on their backs. Several little white dogs followed along. They were heading south on the huckleberry plains to pick huckleberries.

The Indians would catch fish in the lakes and take them back in the country and trade them for pork and flour. Above Barker Creek were a lot of Irish immigrants of the Catholic faith. One old Indian would peddle fish up there and pretend he was a good Catholic, but when he got down around Mabel among the Protestants, he pretended to be a good Protestant.

The Saginaw Trail used by the Indians came up from Saginaw across Kalkaska County and along the east side of Whitewater Township in Grand Traverse County along the west side of Round Lake on Skegemog Point and ended at the shore of Elk Lake. The Indians measured their distance in days. Ask an Indian how far it was to Saginaw, he would say so many days; or so many days to Detroit.

TRAVERSE BAY LAND OFFICE
—AT—
Elk Rapids, - - - Michigan.

A General Land business transacted in

Fruit, Pine and Farming Lands.

The interests of Resident and Non-resident Land owners attended to in the Grand Traverse Region. Lands Examined Platted and valued for owners or purchasers by a competent Surveyor.

We own the only Abstracts of Title to all Lands in

Antrim, Kalkaska, Otsego and Crawford COUNTIES,

Accurately written up with all defects carefully noted. Abstracts furnished and Titles perfected on reasonable terms

To Capitalists, Superior facilities for Investments in carefully selected lands are offered at rates which will guarantee security and profit.

Below will be found a partial list of lands now offered for sale at this office Correspondence or personal application will receive prompt attention.

GEO. E. STEELE,   WILLIAMS & PARKINSON,
   Surveyor.   Attorneys and Commissioners.

Figure 1.1: 1873 Elk Rapids newspaper advertisement
Courtesy of Glenn Neumann

Recollections

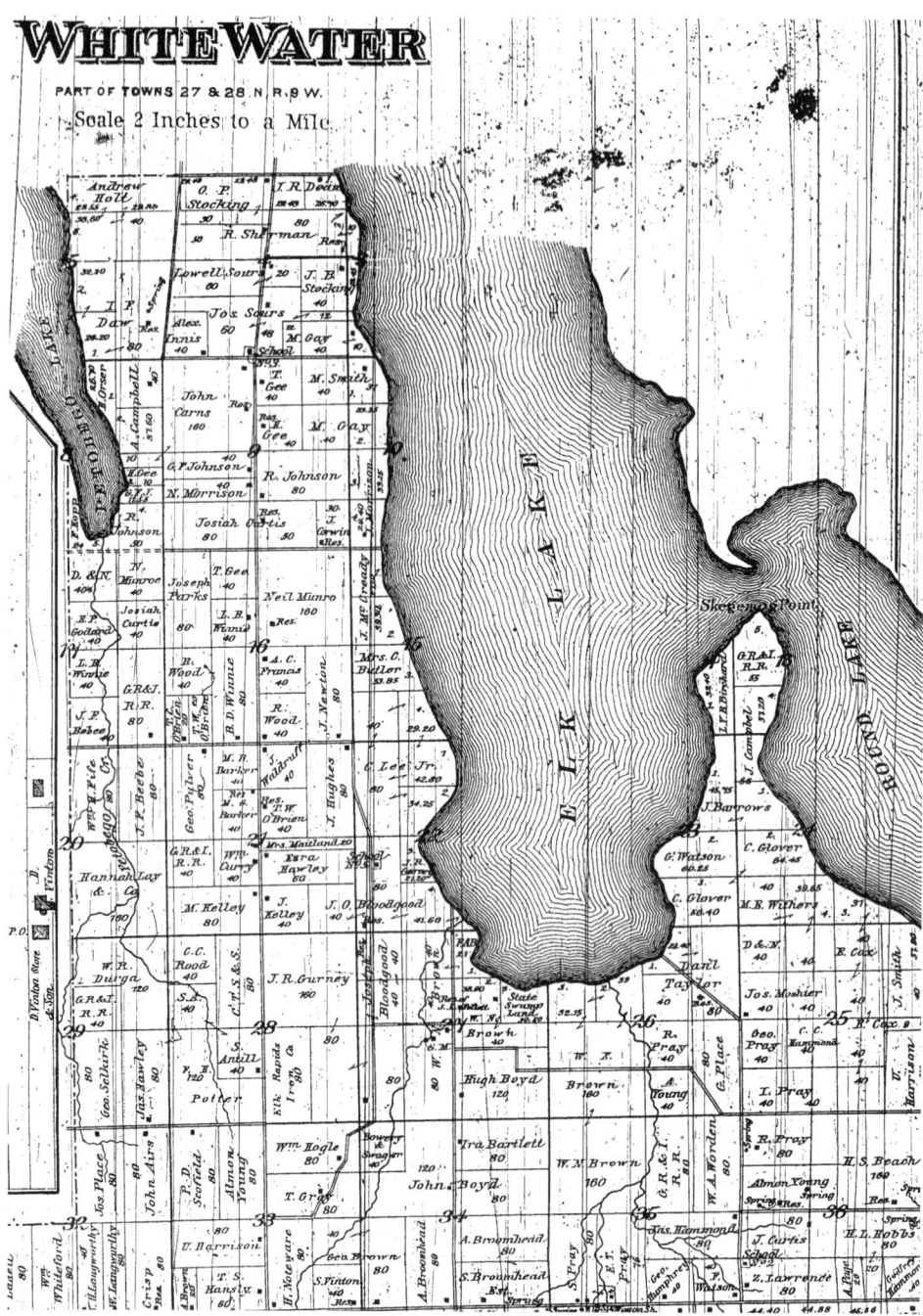

Figure 1.2: 1881 Land Map of Whitewater Township

Whitewater Township

Whitewater Township was organized in 1859. It contained Acme and part of East Bay Township. William H. Fife was the first Supervisor.

East Bay Township was organized in 1867 by the Board of Supervisors. It included a portion of the present township of Acme and a resident of that portion, J. B. Haviland, was the first Supervisor. This was also a part of the original township of Whitewater.

Acme Township was organized in January of 1891 from part of East Bay Township, which was originally part of Whitewater Township. John Pulcipher was the first Supervisor of Acme Township.

Acme Township, I believe, went by the name of East Bay from 1867 when it was separated from Whitewater Township 'til 1891 when East Bay was divided, the south part remaining East Bay and the north part taking the name of Acme.

In 1889 Whitewater Township built a Town Hall at Williamsburg at a cost of $800.00. It was still in use in 1985.

The northeast corner of Whitewater laid across the narrows between Elk and Round Lakes consisted of Sections 1 and 2, and 11 and 12, town 28, north range 9 west. Only Section 1 is a full section of land. The other sections lay partly in the lakes. Since the people in these sections of land would have to go clear around the north end of Elk Lake or clear around Round Lake to get to the rest of Whitewater Township by land to vote or any other official business, this part of the township was attached to Antrim County.

Whitewater Township

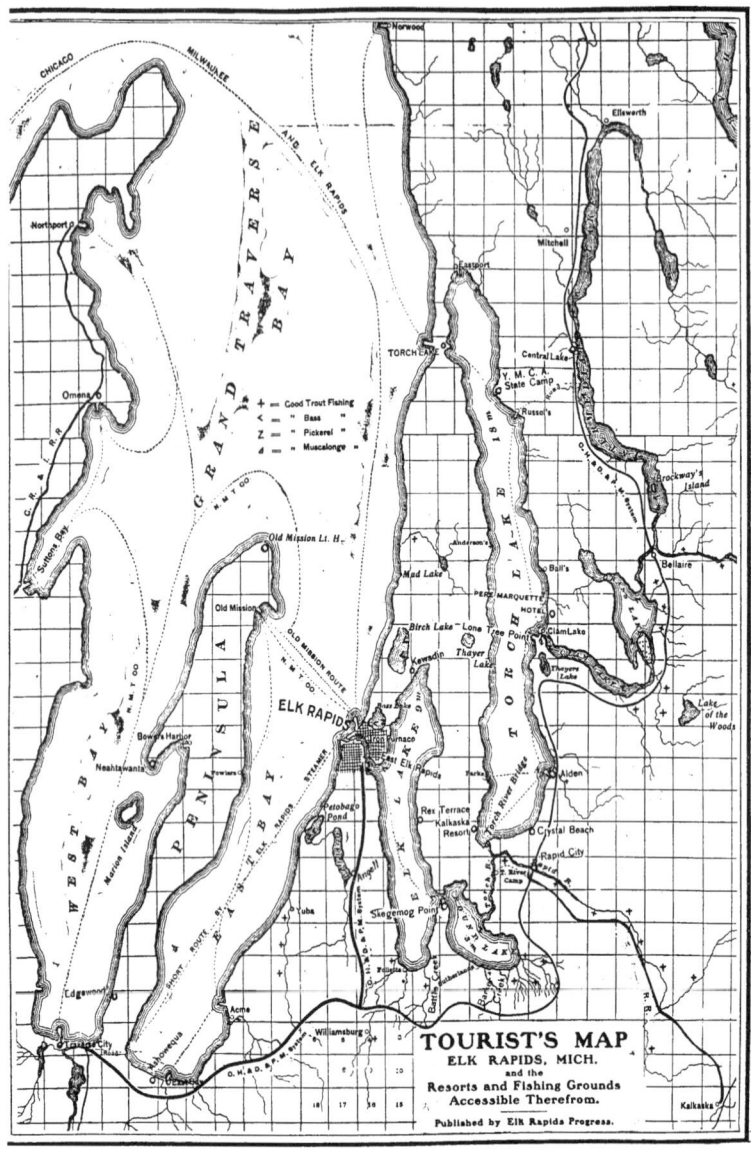

Figure 1.3: 1905 Tourist Map
Courtesy of Elk Rapids Area Historical Society

First Post Office for Whitewater Township

The first Post Office was called Whitewater. It was located where Acme now is. An Indian by the name of Philip Post carried mail from there through on what is now M-72 and on up to Petoskey. He rode a pony, but when the pony drowned crossing a river up north, he carried it on foot. You could put up a box along the route and give him a dollar and he would put your mail in it for a year. There were other Indians who also carried mail.

In 1867 the first Post Office was established at what is now Williamsburg. It was called Dunbar with a man named Eber J. Dunbar as Postmaster. Williamsburg was called Mill Creek before it was called Dunbar. In 1869 the name was changed from Dunbar to Williamsburg and a man by the name of C. C. Williams was named postmaster. It was also called Williamsburgh for a while.

Also in 1869, the name of the Whitewater Post Office at Acme was changed to Acme with A. Hoxsie as Postmaster.

In 1867 a stage ran from Dunbar post office to Elk Rapids, going out and returning each Monday and Thursday to carry the mail. Passengers and some freight were also carried. A stage ran from Acme to Barker Creek after a post office was established at Barker Creek in 1874 to carry the mail. This stage ran once a week at first. In the 1880's it was extended to twice a week. Barker Creek was a little town east of the county line in Kalkaska County. In the later 1880's the mail was carried by stage three times a week from Acme to Barker Creek.

When the railroad came through in 1892, the mail was then carried on the train.

First Post Office

Figure 1.4: Gristmill Pond at Williamsburg about 1910
Courtesy of Kim Acker

Figure 1.5: Trout Hatchery at Mill Pond
Courtesy of Kathi Waggoner Gober

Gristmills and Sawmills in Whitewater

Charles Truman and Laura Scofield came to Whitewater Township in 1861 and settled at what is now Williamsburg (according to Sprague's History of Grand Traverse and Leelanau Counties). They established a grist mill where they made flour for the settlers from the wheat grown in the community. This was a stone grind mill. He also had a sawmill making lumber. These mills ran for many years by water power from the pond made by damming up the Williamsburg Creek.

When Scofield built the grist mill and started grinding flour, the settlers held a celebration. It was a big thing when they could raise their own wheat and get it ground into flour for their food and not have to bring their flour in from outside by boat. Before this, some of the settlers had a coffee mill they would grind wheat in to make flour. They would lend it to their neighbors.

Also according to Sprague's History, H. A. Langworthy's father came to Williamsburg in 1854 and built a sawmill which he operated until 1857. Amon Langworthy was the name of the Langworthy who came to Williamsburg in 1854. I do not know if this is the sawmill that Scofield took over and ran, or if he built one of his own.

These mills were located south of Church Street between the street and the pond. The grist mill was on the west side of the Williamsburg Creek and the sawmill on the east side of the creek. These mills have been torn down for many years. There is still a small building on the west side of the creek where the grist mill was, which may have been used in the flour grinding operation.

In 1878 according to Charley Eaton and Wilbur Stites, Charley's father, A. W. Eaton, arrived to take over the job as manager of the Scofield's mills. He was a skillful operator and turned out more grist and cut more board feet of lumber than ever before.

One of the best men in the sawmill at the time was Kossuth Stites. He could file a big saw, scale a load of logs, cruise a piece of timber, or any of the other jobs around a mill.

Gristmills and Sawmills

Figure 1.6: Kossuth Stites Sharpening Mill Saw Blade
Courtesy of Grand Traverse Pioneer and Historical Society

Eaton and Stites decided there was room for another sawmill in Williamsburg. They talked it over with David Vinton, another resident of the community, and he decided to venture with them. He was never an active partner in the Eaton and Stites Mill, but had an undisclosed amount of capital invested.

The site chosen for the new sawmill was east of the present Village of Williamsburg on the south side of the old M-72, but on the north side of the new 72 between the Vinton Road and the Williamsburg Road. A flowing well was drilled to supply water for the boilers which is still flowing just north of the railroad embankment. A small house sits near this well now. This was a mill run by steam power.

The railroad was not built yet when the mill was built. When the railroad did come through in 1892, they built it on a trestle over the mill yard so teams could haul loads of logs under the track. When the mill was torn down in 1904, the railroad was filled in under the track with dirt to make the present embankment. The mill machinery was shipped by rail from Kalamazoo to Traverse City and brought the rest of the way by horse team. The death of A. W. Eaton in 1888 ended the profitable partnership. The mill was then purchased by Dave Vinton and son. Kossuth Stites remained on as superintendent. It ran for a few years, and was then sold to Albert Devries, who ran it 'til 1904. It was then torn down. Kossuth Stites directed the destruction of the mill which he had helped to build. This ended the lumbering era in Williamsburg.

On Battle Creek east of Williamsburg near where Linnie Pray's house stood in 1986, a man named William R. Durga had a sawmill and also a shingle mill. An embankment can still be seen here from the new M-72 road where they had a pond. However, I believe this mill was run by a steam engine as I do not believe there was enough power from this creek. This mill used what was called a muley saw, a straight blade which ran up and down like a jigsaw. This saw was much slower than the circle saw in cutting lumber. Not nearly as many board feet of lumber could be cut in a day. Mr. Durga also owned 600 acres of land in East Bay, now Acme Township, where he lived and farmed it in addition to lumbering.

Another man by the name of Len Rickerd had a blacksmith shop here. He also made coffins for the settlers. He made a coffin for my grandfather out of black cherry for the sum of five dollars.

Across the road on the north side of what is now Old M-72 another man by the name of Clement had a shingle mill.

In 1867 a Mr. Plat built a sawmill farther down the Williamsburg Creek toward Elk Lake. It was also driven by water power.

J. I. Follett with his son James S. Follett came to the Grand Traverse region in 1871 and bought a mill and several hundred acres of land at the south end of Elk Lake. Whether this was the sawmill that Plat built I am not sure, but the Follett mill was in this same area. They ran this mill for several years. They operated a brick yard in Elk Rapids while they rebuilt the sawmill. The Folletts, both father and son, enlisted

Gristmills and Sawmills

in the Civil War on December 4, 1861 in the same Twelfth Michigan Infantry and served all through the war. Both were wounded at the battle of Shiloh, the father remaining ill for the rest of his life.

Another sawmill south of Williamsburg was A. Campeau's mill, formerly Dodd's Mill. It was destroyed by fire in 1887 and rebuilt. There were other sawmills in the township, some southwest of Williamsburg, one owned by C. T. Scofield and sons. In the later 1920's and early 1930's Milton Beckwith had a sawmill and did custom sawing for the people. In the 1940's and early 50's Lewis Palmer had a sawmill and did custom sawing.

When father was yet small in the 1870's, the State hired men to chop a road from Acme through to Harrisburg on Lake Huron along what is now M-72. A man by the name of Oscar Noble was boss of this West end. Another man had the East end to look after.

The timber in this region was cut and hauled to the bank of Elk and Round Lake. It had to be hauled with oxen in the early days as there were no horses 'til later. There were not many horses brought in before the later 1870's.

Wirt Dexter, and Henry and Ed Noble had a sawmill at Elk Rapids. They also had several lumber camps around the lakes, some run by Michael Gay, cutting these logs. When they got the logs to the lakes, they floated them down to Elk Rapids where they sawed them into lumber.

Gristmills and Sawmills

Figure 1.7: Williamsburg Mill
Courtesy Grand Traverse Pioneer and Historical Society

Figure 1.8: Mill Race at Williamsburg
Courtesy of Kathi Waggoner Gober

Gristmills and Sawmills

Figure 1.9: Pioneer Farm
Courtesy of Gloria Wiltzer

Figure 1.10: Haywagon
George Watson on wagon, unidentified man and Upsall Cox on ground
Courtesy of Samels Collection

Business and Farming in Whitewater

In 1872 Wirt Dexter and the Nobles formed a company known as the Elk Rapids Iron Company and built a blast furnace there to smelt the iron. They brought the ore in from Escanaba by boat.

The settlers then cut cord wood and sold it to the company to make into charcoal to smelt the iron. Cord wood was cut four feet long. They hauled it to the bank of the lakes in the winter, and in the spring it was loaded on scows and towed by steam tug to Elk Rapids.

Father hauled all one winter from Mabel down to the old Taylor landing on Elk Lake. By spring he had quite a piece of the flat around the landing covered. After the railroads came through in 1892, he hauled and loaded it on cars at Mabel. He loaded 48 cars there one winter. When the train came along it hauled them to Elk Rapids. They did not get much money for timber in those days. Cord wood sold for 75 cents a cord of 4 ft. wood. Best logs were $1.25 a thousand board foot. Standing timber on the stump sold for 50 cents a thousand. One 40 acres of pine on the plains estimated at 50 cents a thousand on the stump brought $10,000.

The Elk Rapids Iron Company had scows built about 18 feet wide by 60 feet long with about 4 or 5 foot high sides decked over. They were made of 3 or 4 inch planks. They brought them up the lake and loaded the cord wood on and hauled them by steam tugs to Elk Rapids. They had one scow with a two story cook shanty built right on the scow where they boarded the men who loaded the scows.

The Iron Company had three of these steam tugs to haul the scows; one called the Elk Lake, one the Torch Lake, the other the Albatross. Fred Laubscher was Captain of the tug Albatross for a few years. When he became ill and could not run it any longer, my Uncle William Samels, Jr. was hired as Captain. Samels was Captain for about 15 years in the latter part of the 1800's and early part of the 1900's. My father told me that this cord wood was hauled to Elk Rapids where it was stood on end with another tier on top, perhaps three tiers high, then covered with dirt and set fire to make it into charcoal. They then hired

Business and Farming

men with teams and wagons with big boxes to haul it to the furnace.

Figure 1.11: Austin Pray plowing with Ed Pray's team
Courtesy of Ada Goss

Figure 1.12: Bernie Scofield and Sylvia with team
Courtesy of Kathi Waggoner Gober

The logs were rolled into the water where they were surrounded by long poles called boom poles chained together. They were then towed by steam tug to Elk Rapids. They were towed down Torch Lake this way and let loose into Torch River to float down the river with booms stretched around the mouth of Torch River in Round Lake to catch them, then towed the rest of the way to Elk Rapids by tug.

There was a rapids in the Elk River at Elk Rapids which gave the town its name. The rapids held the water in Elk and Round Lakes up higher than the Bay. There was also mention of a cliff here that the water flowed over, and a mention of blue clay here that held the lakes up. Sometime in the 1860's they built a dam below the rapids to get power to run the sawmill. It raised the water in the lakes about 28 inches. This caused considerable wash around the shores and head of the lakes. Before putting in this dam they held a hearing and several of the settlers went down, including Dave Vinton, to discuss the effects of the dam on the lakes.

Before the dam was built, the water across the narrows between Elk and Round Lakes was shallow enough so that my grandfather, Captain William Samels, Sr. (he was a Captain in the mines of England and Canada), could wade across by holding his clothes above his head. He was a short man.

One of the first major events in the community was the building of a grist mill at Williamsburg by Truman Scofield. The Williamsburg Creek was dammed to get power for the grist mill and sawmill. They built the grist mill, but they had to have some bunting to bolt the flour through before it could be made into bread. So a couple of the women were sent to Canada to get the bunting. They made it into a petticoat and wore it across the border so as not to have to pay duty on it. When I speak of going to Canada, south of here was all wilderness yet with no settlers 'til you got almost to Grand Rapids, and no roads. If you went that way you had to go afoot and make your own trail. It took six days to walk from Traverse City to Grand Rapids. One party got lost and it took them nine days. All the early settlers came in by boat, mostly from Detroit up through the Straits of Mackinac, then on to Elk Rapids or Old Mission or Northport.

Business and Farming

Figure 1.13: Threshing at Orin Lindsey's, Mabel
Courtesy of Kathi Waggoner Gober

When the mill was done and the first grist was ground, they had a day of celebration as this was a great step forward in the community when the people could raise their own wheat and corn and get it ground into flour for bread and cornmeal. Cornmeal was a staple food in the pioneer days. Instead of charging money for grinding, they took out so much flour, which they called toll.

When father was quite young, his folks sent him to the mill with the oxen and a bushel of wheat on a stoneboat to get ground. Mr. Scofield asked him if he could lift the bag of wheat from the stoneboat up onto the platform of the mill. He said he couldn't, so Mr. Scofield picked up the bag and carried it into the mill. He then asked father to get on the scales and he weighed him. He said no wonder he could not lift the bag of wheat as he only weighed three pounds more than a bushel of wheat.

One summer they got short of wheat before thrashing time and Mr. Copeland thrashed first. He came along with his horse and buggy and dropped a bag off at the gate of some of the settlers who were short.

Grain had to be cut by hand with a cradle swung by a strong man and laid in swaths, then tied by hand with a twist of straw in the early days 'til the reaper was invented, which cut it and laid it in swaths. It still had to be tied by hand 'til finally the binder was invented which cut and tied it in one operation.

Thrashing was also done by hand with flails on the barn floor and fanned out in the wind. Flails were made of two sticks, one longer for a handle and a shorter one to flail the grain tied together with a leather strap or thong.

The first thrashing machines that came into the country were run by horse power, which consisted of a center swivel with sweeps to hitch a team on. The horses went around and around the center with tumbling rods to transfer the power to the cylinder of the thrashing machine. The horses had to step over the tumbling rods as they went around. Some machines required four horses and some eight. These machines required three teams to move from place to place. One team hauled the separator, one team the power, and one team the trap wagon which had the tumbling rods piled on. Every 40 acre farm had a thrashing, so there would be several machines going all fall to do the thrashing.

After the horse power with sweeps, the steam engine was invented and was used to run the threshing maching. Then the gasoline engine was invented, and the gasoline tractor to run the threshing machines.

Hay also had to be cut by hand with a scyth and raked by hand 'til the horse drawn mowing machines and rakes came into the country. This was along in the 1880's about the same time as the reaper was invented, and a little later the binder was invented.

Farming was quite a business in Whitewater Township in the early days, along with the logging. The farmers would work their farms in the summer and take their teams of horses to the lumber camps in

Business and Farming

the winter, or they would cut cord wood to sell to the furnace in Elk Rapids. They would haul this wood to the lake shore in the winter and the company would load it on their scows in the spring and summer and tow it down the lakes with their steam tugs. After the railroad came through in 1892, they would haul it to the railroad and load it on the cars to be hauled by locomotive to Elk Rapids.

Figure 1.14: Potato Loading
Courtesy of Karon Anderson

The first main crop they raised was wheat. The next was potatoes. Now it is cherries. The land was new and it produced good crops for awhile. A few of these farms were only 40 acres. Many were 80 acres and a few were larger. As there was quite a bit of hand labor in farming in the early days, there were quite a few men hired to help on the farms.

Most every farm of more than 40 acres would have a hired man or two. The larger farms would have more. The hired men would work on the farms in the summer and take the farmer's team to the logging camps in the winter, or else help the farmer cut cordwood in the winters.

Wages for a hired man on the farm would run about $20 a month and board. Some of the women would have a hired girl to help with the housework as there was a lot of work to do in the house to feed the men, and most of it had to be done by hand. As a rule the farmers would have larger families, which made a lot of work.

In the very early days, the farming and logging were done by oxen 'til they began to get horses along in the 1870's. From the 1880's on it was done with horses 'til the 1920's when the farmers began to get tractors.

In addition to wheat and potatoes, each farm had a herd of cattle, a size to fit the size of the farm. Many of them also had a flock of sheep and a few hogs. For the first half of the 1900's the main product the farmers had to sell was cream. There were two cream stations in Williamsburg at one time buying cream. There were several cream stations in Traverse City.

To keep meat and stuff cold, some of the early settlers would cut cakes of ice from the lakes in the winter, and store it in sheds. They packed sawdust from the sawmills around it. The sawdust would be about a foot thick on the sides and over the top. This would keep the ice from melting for the summer.

The farmers in the early days bought their wagons and sleighs in Traverse City and Elk Rapids. There were several shops in Traverse City and Elk Rapids building wagons and sleighs for the farmers and also Big Wheels and sleighs for the lumbering industry. (see picture page 30)

In Traverse City, Caldwell and Louden made wagons and sleighs for the farms, and Big Wheels for the lumbering industry. These Big Wheels were shipped as far south as Texas and Georgia. A. J. Petertyl and Company made wagons for the farmers. Victor Petertyl made carriages.

Business and Farming

Broadfoot and Carrier was another company that made Big Wheels for the lumbering industry. They shipped many Big Wheels south to Grand Rapids and around. They made what was called the Broadfoot Wagon for the farmers. They also sold farm machinery to the farmers.

G. F. Murray apparently made wagons as he advertised for birch blocks for hubs for wheels. There were also many shops in Traverse City making harnesses for the farmers horses.

Wilhelm, Bartok and Company made harnesses. Beadle was another shop making harnesses. The Beadle Building still stands on the northwest corner of Front and Cass Street in Traverse City occupied by a microbrewery in the late 1990s.

Howard Whiting sold farm machinery in Traverse City to the farmers. Lue Rice also sold farm machinery in Traverse City.

Some farmers raised their own horses but they could also buy horses in Traverse City. Clark and Birney J. Morgan sold horses in Traverse City. Tom Shane and Howard Whiting sold horses there also. There were several blacksmith shops in Traverse City.

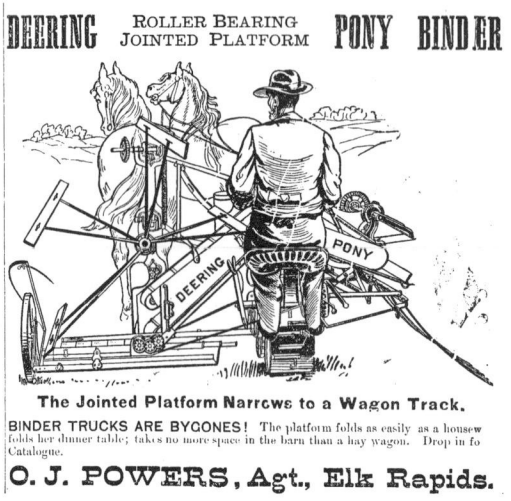

Figure 1.15: 1896 Elk Rapids newspaper advertisement
Courtesy of Glenn Neumann

Business and Farming

In Elk Rapids John E. Cooper had a shop where he made wagons as early as 1869. Martin Kramer had a blacksmith shop in Elk Rapids where he made and repaired wagons, buggies and sleighs and shoed horses. Another man by the name of, I believe, Rob Rex made wagons in Elk Rapids. Either Kramer or Rex made a wagon for our step-grandfather, Adolf Kaiser, in the 1880's. We have the wagon yet. One would make it for $55, the other for $60. The one that would make it for $55 got the job of making the wagon. I believe that included the box and all. Charley Beebe had a blacksmith shop in Elk Rapids in the early 1900's. There were other blacksmith shops in Elk Rapids in the last half of the 1800's.

We had a blacksmith and woodworking shop on our farm on the Skegemog Point Road. Dennis and Ben Samels repaired farm machinery and did other blacksmith work such as making grab hooks and chain links in the later 1920's and 30's, and in the early 1940's during World War II when farm tools were hard to get. They did woodwork here too. They also made fish spears for the fishermen. Ben made over 200 fish spears 'til he had to quit on account of his heart. I made cabinets and did other woodwork in this shop also.

Figure 1.16: James Watson packing apples
Courtesy of Ada Goss

Business and Farming

Figure 1.17: Train at Bates Station
Courtesy of Kathi Waggoner Gober

Figure 1.18: Train at Williamsburg Station
Courtesy of Grand Traverse Pioneer and Historical Society

Railroads

The first and only railroad through Whitewater Township was the Chicago and West Michigan. It came through in 1892. They graded the right of way the year before and I believe laid the rails into Elk Rapids, on New Years Day of 1892. The first train ran into Elk Rapids. My father, Frank Samels, and a man named Emery Rose, who lived around Williamsburg, bought the first tickets in Williamsburg to go to Elk Rapids. They cut the tickets out of a shoebox. The summer of 1892 they laid the rails from Williamsburg on through Barker Creek, Rapid City and on up north.

Around 1900 the Pere Marquette Railroad Company took over this railroad and ran it for almost half a century. Then the Chesapeake and Ohio Railroad took it over and ran it 'til it was abandoned in the early 1980's. Now the rails have been taken up except for a short strip from Williamsburg to Grawn, which was bought by the State of Michigan and is served by what was the Old Grand Rapids and Indiana railroad branch from Walton Junction to Traverse City.

When the first railroads came through Whitewater Township in 1892, there was much lumbering in the area, although many of the logs had been cut in the Township. There was still a lot of timber to be cut to the east and north of the Township and along the Boardman River. This made a lot of work for the railroads, hauling logs and cord wood. Some logs were hauled to Elk Rapids to the Dexter and Noble sawmill. Also cord wood was hauled to Elk Rapids for the furnace built by Dexter and Noble to smelt iron.

From 1892 'til the 1920's the railroads were very busy in the area. At one time there were four passenger trains a day, two each way. There was one at 6 A.M. and one at 11 A.M. going south and one at 2 P.M. and 6 P.M. going north. They kept a locomotive at Williamsburg just to haul the cars into Elk Rapids.

They had a water tank on a tower at Williamsburg to supply water for the steam locomotives on the railroads. This tank was kept full by Arch Gardiner from a well on his property. He was a local well

Railroads

driller. This was in the teens and twenty's. Later they took the tank out and got their water at other stations. What they did for water before Gardiners moved there, I do not know. They used the steam locomotives on the railroads 'til the Chesapeake and Ohio Railroad took it over sometime in the later 1940's. I believe it was in 1947 or 1951. Then they put on diesel engines.

It was said at one time there were eleven trains a day going into Elk Rapids, including the passenger trains, the logging trains, and trains hauling cordwood. After the cement plant was built in the late 1890's at Elk Rapids, they hauled stone from Petoskey to Elk Rapids to make cement from. They had to haul coal in for the cement plant and for the people to burn. They also hauled out the farmers' produce and hauled in whatever supplies the farmers and other people needed. There was also much work for the railroads to do to the north, both passenger trains and freight trains through to Petoskey and all the towns along the way. There was much timber that way too.

There were many carloads of potatoes to be hauled from Elk Rapids, Williamsburg, Bates and some from Barker Creek, a few from Mabel and some from Angell, a little town between Williamsburg and Elk Rapids on the Elk Rapids track. Some beans were also hauled from Williamsburg and Elk Rapids. The busiest time for the railroads, for logs and cord wood, was from 1892 'til the mid teens when the sawmill and furnace at Elk Rapids closed down. The saw timber was all cut and gone which caused the sawmill to shut down. And when the cord wood was all gone, it was not profitable for the furnace to run as they had to haul the iron ore across Lake Michigan by boat from Escanaba, so it shut down.

"Tunk" was a side track on the Chicago and West Michigan Railroad, later the Pere Marquette. It was located between the Skegemog and Baggs Road in Whitewater Township, Grand Traverse County. In 1890 or '91 a cement plant was built in Elk Rapids to make cement out of the marl in Petobego Lake between Elk Rapids and Yuba. But this marl did not prove suited for cement. So they hauled limestone from Petoskey by the railroad. They could haul quite long strings of cars from Petoskey to near Barker Creek, but a little upgrade made it hard to pull them farther. So they split the train here and took part of the cars up to this sidetrack. That was the reason for building this sidetrack. They would then go back with the engine and get the rest of the cars. In going up this grade as they crossed the joints in the rails they would make a noise that sounded like "tunk, tunk, tunk." So that is how they came to call this side track Tunk.

In 1910 it was the stone train from Petoskey that came head-on with another train on the Skegemog Road crossing.

The cement plant at Elk Rapids shut down in 1911 because it was not profitable to haul stone clear from Petoskey. But apparently the railroads still hauled limestone downstate.

Potatoes and beans were hauled for the farmers from 1892 'til along in the 1920's and some 'til World War II when some of the farmers went to raising cherries. When the manufacturing plants came into Traverse City during World War II, it gave the farmers work which was more profitable than raising crops. Some livestock was also hauled on the railroads during this time.

The passengers on the railroads began to taper off when the automobile came in. They cut down to one train a day each way. The mail kept them going for a while but when the Government took the mail off the trains and put it on the trucks, it was unprofitable for them to run so they took the passenger trains off the railroads. The last passenger out of Traverse City was on October 19, 1966. The freight trains kept on running 'til February 20, 1982, two or three trains a week.

During the busy part of the railroad era, they ran a resort special called the Flyer to carry the resorters up north, one train from Detroit and one from Chicago. You could get on these trains in the evening at Detroit or Chicago and be up here in the morning, or get on the trains here in the evening and be back at Detroit or Chicago in the morning. These trains ran on weekends and holidays and maybe every day, I am not sure. I don't know when they started these trains, but they ran in the teens and early twenties. These trains ran as far as Petoskey. They ran during the summer months.

Railroads

Figure 1.19: 1903 Island Lake Lumber Camp Crew with Big Wheels
From left: Helen Pray Watson (camp cook) with baby John, unidentified woman, Jim Watson with daughter Ada, unidentified man, Pat Boyd, three unidentified men, Jack Boyd (Pat's son) sitting on the big wheel.
Courtesy of Carl Goss

Lumbering in Whitewater

Logging Camps

There were several logging camps along the Boardman River. Father worked in two or three of them.

The settlers would take their teams of horses out in the fall after the snow got deep enough for good sledding, and stay all winter hauling logs, boarding in the camps. They would haul logs all day and pile them in the river and at midnight a man would let the dam out at South Boardman. By morning the water would have carried the logs down toward Traverse City.

Sometimes they would bank the logs in piles along the river bank with a toggle holding the key log. They would have a pit dug ahead of the logs big enough for a man to get into and knock the toggle out and let the logs roll down over him into the river. Something went wrong one of these times and the man got killed. I believe this happened on the Manistee River.

Island Lake Camp

The Island Lake lumber camp, about 4 miles southeast of Mabel and Barker Creek, was owned by the Elk Rapids Iron Company. It was located a little ways north of Island Lake in Wilson Township, Kalkaska County. Wilson Township was later consolidated with Kalkaska Township in Kalkaska County. There was also a wood camp here with men cutting wood for the Elk Rapids Iron company. They ran a railroad from Kalkaska to get the logs and wood out.

The windmill at the Island Lake Camp was later bought by Walter Watson and moved to their hotel at Torch River bridge. Later when he got an electric pump, he sold the windmill to my father, Frank Samels. Frank took it down and set it up on our farm on the Skegemog Point Road where it still stands.

Lumbering

Walt Watson was foreman; Harry Farrell was bookkeeper. Some of the Whitewater Township people who worked around there were William Samels, Jr., Howard Brown, Philip Ray, Tom Dockery, Gervas Watson and some of the Boyds. There were more.

Island Lake Lumber Camp was operated by the Elk Rapids Iron Company. Walter Watson was foreman, his wife Maggie worked as a camp cook, and they ran the company store. The Watsons and their daughter Dorothy lived in upper left cabin.

Figure 1.20: Island Lake Lumber Camp, 1903
Courtesy of Carl Goss

Lumber Camps of Whitewater

Hannah and Lay Lumbermen of Traverse City had several logging camps along the Boardman River. Father worked in two of them hauling logs one winter. He had a $400 team of horses. The second winter he and two other men with teams were hired to tow the other teams hauling logs up the hills. They got paid by the day and found, meaning board and lodging. These two camps were located one on Randolph Lake, the other nearby.

In another camp owned by Cobb and Mitchell, two lumbermen from Cadillac, there were many Canadian French men working. Father worked here awhile another winter but did not like it here and quit. Paynes was another camp.

There were several other camps. I have heard of some but do not recall their names. One was along the Williamsburg Road on the way to the river. Dexter and Noble Lumbermen of Elk Rapids had at least two camps in Whitewater Township, one on Round Lake in Section 24 on the Skegemog Point, another on the Baggs Road in Section 25. Michael Gay ran these camps for the company. This was at a very early date, the early 1860's or before. There were other camps including one at the head of Elk Lake where they squared timbers.

John Toirrents had a lumber camp west of the Fife Lake Road, now called the Williamsburg Road. This camp was known as Smith's camp. They had 60 men, 20 teams of horses and five yoke of oxen working in 1887.

A large amount of cedar was cut at the heads of Elk and Round Lakes and shipped to Chicago in 1884 to be made into furniture.

Wages in the lumber camp were $2.00 a day for man and team and found, which meant board and lodging for man and team.

In the two camps father worked in for Hannah and Lay they had good cooks. One winter they had a man cook, the other they had a woman cook and her husband helped around the camp. Father had

Lumbering

high praise for the food they got in these camps as Perry Hannah said the better they fed the men, the better they would work. They had all beef for meat, no pork.

They had a table set in the camp with pie and doughnuts on it. Whenever the men with teams went by the camp they could go in and get a piece of pie or doughnut. They used lots of seasoning in their food, especially cinnamon in their apple pie, which father liked.

Some of the other camps did not feed as good and on Sundays, some of their men would come to Hannah's camp and get a meal. Any strangers or tramps who came to the camp, they would put them up for the night and give them a meal.

These camps had a blacksmith there to shoe the horses so they could pull on the ice, as they would sprinkle the roads with water to freeze so the sleigh would slip easier and they could haul bigger loads. Some of these blacksmiths were not so good, however. In one camp where father worked there was a good blacksmith worked as a laborer. Some of the men on Sunday would break into the regular blacksmith's shop and get this man to shoe their horses because he would do a better job. He could polish the shoes and make them look like silver. They asked him why he worked for a dollar a day in the camp when he could make more in town working at his trade. He said if he worked in town he would work all day and go to the saloon at night and drink it all up. Out in the camp he could save his money.

The sleighs they used were made very wide with 12 foot bunks. They would roll the logs on these bunks 'til full and pile more on top 'til they would be as big as a load of hay.

They sprinkled water on the roads to freeze to make them like ice. One team with sharp shoes on could pull these big loads on the level, but when they came to a hill they would put another team on to tow them up the hills.

The first lumbering in Whitewater Township was done around Round Lake in 1851. Lumbering then crept southward year by year 'til about

1890 when they were clear out to the Boardman River. This first lumbering was done with teams of oxen, then later with teams of horses. Some horses were used, I believe, in the 1860's and from then on it was more with horses than oxen.

There were no bulldozers then. These logs all had to be cut by hand with two men, one on each end of a cross cut saw. There were no chain saws then.

Square Timber Camp

Father went out east to Manistee Lake one fall to haul square timber. They had a lot of Frenchmen with big wide broad axes hewing these big pine into square timbers. This was hand work. One stock he saw was 90 feet long, 4 feet square at the butt and 2 feet square at the top. It was hewn so smooth it looked as though it had gone through a planer. It was going to England for a mast for a vessel.

These Frenchmen had a big grindstone in the camp with a crank on each side. A man would sit on each side and turn the stone while they ground their axes. They would be grinding all night long.

Father only stayed one week as they were all strangers except Dell Fairbanks, a neighbor from Mabel. They both left on Sunday morning. Father had to wait for them to make a pair of sleighs for him so he only got in a couple of days hauling, enough to pay for his board for the week. He could have made good money if he had stayed. He came home and went out on the Boardman and got a job in a camp there.

Lumbering

Figure 1.21: Log House
Burl Broomhead, Mr. and Mrs. Bill Cook and unknown
Courtesy of Kathi Waggoner Gober

Figure 1.22: House Roofing Bee at Mabel, 1910
Big Ed Pray, Mrs. Lackey and Ina Lackey on roof of Henry Lackey's Log House
Courtesy of Ina Robb

Log Houses

When the early settlers came into Whitewater Township they built log houses because of the availability of logs and the absence of sawmills to make sawed lumber. As the country became more settled and the sawmills were brought in, they could get sawed lumber and they began to build frame houses.

I remember three of these log houses on the Skegemog Point Road. One was still occupied by my great aunt Sarah Watson, wife of Fielding Benny Watson. This was in the late teens or early twenties. This log house of Fielding Benny Watson was on the south end of Skegemog Road on the west side of the road. One of these log houses was being torn down one day when I was going home from school in the 1920's.

The first frame house built in the eastern part of Whitewater Township was built by Almon Young in either 1868 or 1869. This house was built on the north side of what is now M-72 between the Skegemog Point Road and the Baggs Road.

Captain William Samels, my grandfather, had lumber cut and planned to build a frame house like this one, but he died in 1871 before having it built. His widow had a small house built from the lumber.

The framing of barns was another project of the early settlers. A carpenter would frame the building from timbers to be put together with wooden pins. They would then have a bee when all the neighbors would get together and raise the frame. They would then cover the frame with lumber to complete the barn.

Empire Stites was a carpenter who framed barns in the early days. Dennis Samels in the 1930's framed some barns. There were other carpenters who framed barns and did general carpenter work also.

Log Houses

Figure 1.23: Dennis Samels, Fisherman
Courtesy of Samels Collection

Hunting and Fishing

The early settlers did some hunting of deer and small game. As to the deer, there were some here when the first settlers came in. Then they kind of disappeared for awhile, then came back. They came back in the central part of the state first. Then around here, the first deer tracks we saw were in 1936 on our farm. When the deer were scarce around here, some of the settlers would go to the upper peninsula of Michigan to hunt them. They would set up camps for perhaps four or five hunters to stay in.

Some settlers hunted small game birds and rabbits. This hunting for deer and small game was done both for food and pleasure.

As to fishing, the timber would hold the winds back so it was warm enough that they could plant their corn around the 10th of May. Then they would go fishing the next day for pleasure and to get some fish to eat. Some would catch enough to eat, and some would salt some down for future eating so they were not wasted. They would fish in Elk and Round Lakes and also in the creeks.

The picture on the opposite page shows Dennis Samels with a muskelunge he speared through the ice on Round Lake. Dennis, who was born October 4, 1900, liked to fish. He taught himself blacksmithing. In the early 1930's he started making fish spears. In the winter months he would make spears in his blacksmith shop and sold them to fisherman. His brother Ben eventually took over making the spears.

Hunting and Fishing

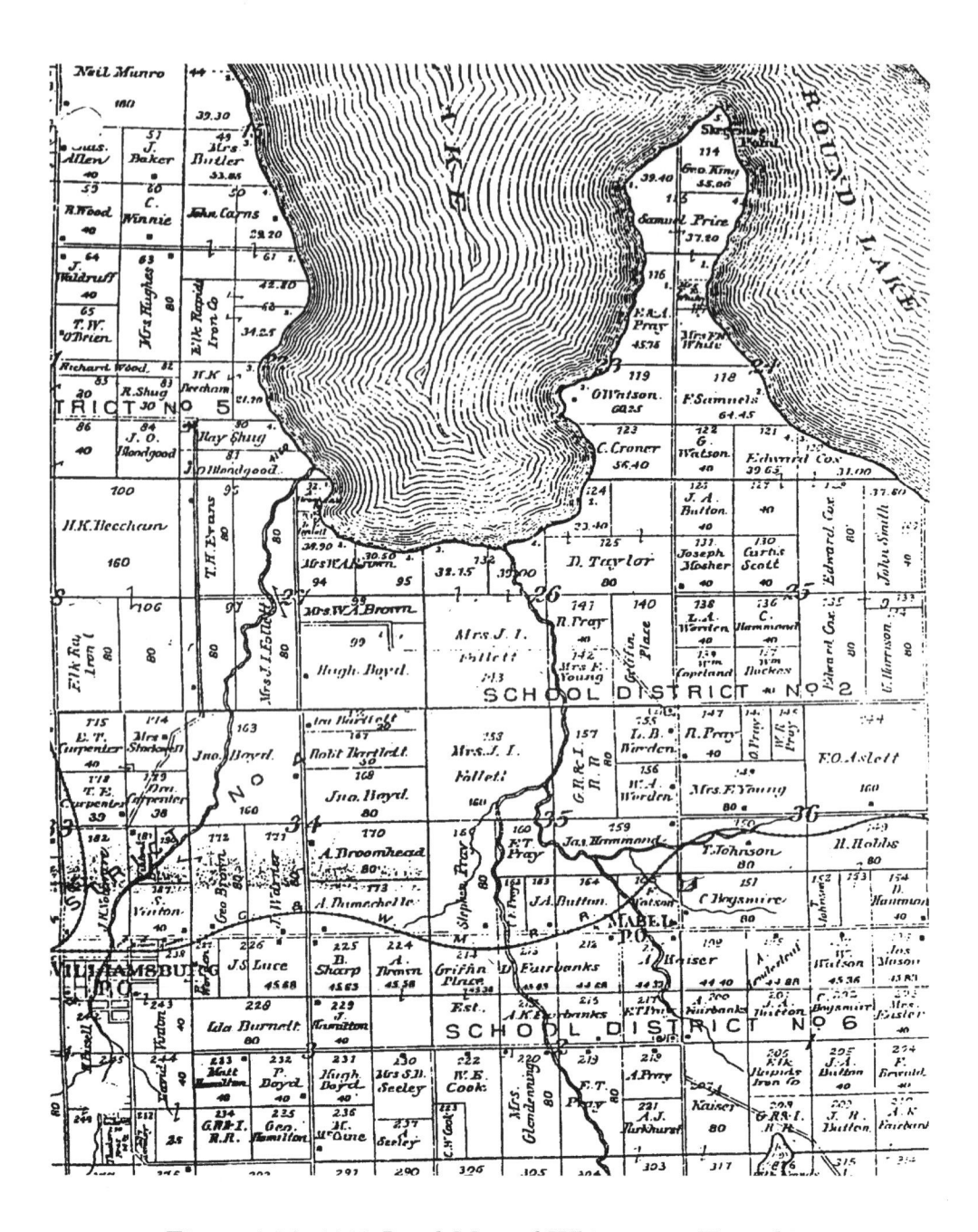

Figure 1.24: 1900 Land Map of Whitewater Township

People of Whitewater Township

Early Settlers

Apparently some of the Langworthys were about the first settlers in Williamsburg itself, coming in 1854 or 55.

But in the outlying area, Joseph Sours came in August of 1855, one of the first settlers in what is the present township of Whitewater. He settled on Section 4, Town 28, North range 9 West. He was the father of Lowell Sours.

The only other settler in the township at this time was a man named Isaac Fundy on Section 15, Town 28, North range 9 West. He died and his family moved away so little is known of him.

In September of 1855 the Watson and Samels families sailed down from Bruce Mines, Ontario. They landed at Skegemog Point and camped there two weeks before moving about two miles south to settle. This included my great-grandfather, Gervas Watson, Sr., and his three sons Fielding (Benny) Watson, William Watson, Gervas Watson, Jr., and daughter Miriam Samels and granddaughter Mary Samels, one year old. His son-in-law Captain William Samels, Sr., who was a Captain in the mines, stayed and worked in the mines up at Bruce Mines a couple of months longer and came down on the last boat in the fall. They also brought a woman of French and Indian descent with them who could talk Indian and also English. They settled on Section 36 just west of the county line and just south of what is now M-72.

H. L. Langworthy, a merchant in Acme, came with his father to Old Mission in Grand Traverse County in 1851. In 1854 his father moved to Williamsburg and built a sawmill which he ran 'til 1857. His name was Amon Langworthy. William Langworthy came in October of 1855.

George Brown was born in New York state in 1833. In 1854 he married Mary Langworthy. The next year 1855 he came with his father-in-law William Langworthy, Philander Odell and a young man named Leavitt to the Grand Traverse region and settled on a farm in Section

People of Whitewater Township

34, Town 28, Range 9. This year witnessed the first permanent settlement of what is now the township of Whitewater.

William Copeland came in the fall of 1855 and settled just over the line in Kalkaska County, becoming the first and only settler in Kalkaska County for many years.

H. L. Beach came in 1856 to East Bay Township. In 1860 he moved to his permanent home in Whitewater in Section 36, Town 28, Range 9 West.

J. M. Merrill came in 1858.

Rev. Daniel B. Scofield came to Williamsburg in about 1860. He was a minister in the Methodist Church here for 35 years. During that time he married 99 couples and presided over many of the funerals. He died in November of 1895. He was the father of ten children, of whom only two survived him. Charles and Daniel were brothers.

Charles Truman and Laura Scofield came to Williamsburg in 1861. They had eleven children who grew up to become quite prominent in the community. Troop Scofield, as he was popularly called, ran the sawmill and grist mill for many years.

A. K. Fairbanks, father of Andrew Fairbanks, came in 1861.

William R. Durga came in 1862 to Whitewater, now Acme Township, and bought 600 acres of land in Section 29 and 32, Town 28, Range 9 West. He also owned a sawmill and shingle mill and eighty-five acres of land in Whitewater Township.

James O. Bloodgood came in 1862. He built the first schoolhouse erected in Williamsburg and installed Miss Sarah Spencer, who later became Mrs. Elvin L. Sprague, as the first teacher.

J. W. Arnold, came to Elk Rapids in 1854 and worked for Dexter & Noble in the sawmill 'til 1868, then bought a farm of eighty acres in Section 31, Town 28, North Range 9 West where he lived the rest of his life. He married Amelia Langworthy in 1865.

David Vinton, Jr. came to Williamsburg about 1870 with his two sons, Frank H. Vinton and Will M. Vinton, and engaged in the mercantile business. His son Frank was his partner. David Vinton Sr. also lived in Whitewater.

J. I. Follett and son James L. Follett came in 1871.

Josiah Curtis moved on his farm in about 1873, which he had purchased in about 1860 in Whitewater. This, I believe, was in Section 36, Town 28.

Other early settlers of Whitewater were Almond Young, James Hammond, Richard Pray, Steve Pray, Ambrose Button, Aaron Broomhead, Dan Taylor, Richard Brown and Art Brown, George Humphrey who was, I believe, grandfather to the Buttons, a man whose last name was Lawrence, Joseph Place, William Fairbanks, Dell Fairbanks, Dr. John White, William Baucus, A. J. Swartout, Adolphus Worden, George Selkirk, Dan B. Scofield, Samuel Seeley, Dr. Springstein, Captain William Samels, Newton Stites, Lafe Rickerd, John Rickerd, Philander Odell, William Merrill, Jack Letherby, John Hamilton, Upsell Harrison, William Pray, Len Rickerd, Mahlon Hoard, Timothy Conant, A. W. Eaton, William Crisp, Vet Cross, Joel Cross, George Broomhead, Lonson Brown, Patrick Boyd, James Boyd, Hugh Boyd, and John Boyd. These four Boyds were brothers. Their mother came with them down from Canada. She was known as Granny Boyd. Kossuth Stites and his brother, Empire Stites. A.K. Fairbanks and his son Andrew Fairbanks. John Carns was another early settler.

In addition to George and Aaron Broomhead, I have heard of a Charley Broomhead who was killed while hauling a load of lumber and the team of horses he was driving balked and tipped the load of lumber over on him.

People of Whitewater Township

The First Generation in Whitewater Township of Grand Traverse County

Town 27 and 28 Range 9 West

These were settlers my father knew and talked about. He was born in 1868 and died in 1955. These were settlers from 1854 through the rest of the 1880's.

Men	Wives
Amon Langworthy	
William Langworthy	Martha (Welton)
Joseph Sours	Mary V. (Lowell)
Isaac Fundy	
Gervas Watson, Sr.	Widower
Fielding (Benny) Watson	Sarah (Lamson)
Capt. William Samels, Sr.	Miriam (Watson)
William Watson	Sarah
Gervas Watson, Jr.	Anne (Hamilton)
A. K. Fairbanks	Mary (Thompson) 1st wife
	Emeline (Eastman) 2nd wife
Andrew Fairbanks	Sarah (Broomhead)
J. M. Merrill	
George Brown	Mary (Langworthy)
Philander Odell	
H. I. Beach	
Josiah Curtis	
David Vinton, Sr.	
David Vinton, Jr.	
Frank Vinton	Emma (Harrison)
Will Vinton	
Medad Vinton	
J. I. Follett, Sr.	
James S. Follett, Jr.	
Almond Young	Emily
James Hammond	Mildred

People of Whitewater Township

Men	Wives
Richard Pray	Melinda
Steve Pray	
George Humphrey	
Ambrose Button	
Jerome Button	
Aaron Broomhead	
Charley Broomhead	
Daniel Taylor	Caroline
Richard (Dick) Brown	Nellie (Vinton)
Art Brown	
Russel Brown	
Am Brown	
Mr. Lawrence	Polly
Joseph Place	
William Fairbanks	
Dell Fairbanks	Doan (Broomhead)
Dr. John White	
A. J. Swartout	
Kossuth Stites	
Empire Stites	
Newton Stites	
J. W. Arnold	Amelia (Langworthy)
William R. Durga	
James O. Bloodgood	Emily B. (Griffis)
John Carns	Lucinda (Hawley)
Matthew Glendenning	Helen (Shaw)
Clement	
Joseph Mosher	Phebe (Taylor)
Vern Worden	
Westen A. Worden	Sarah J.
Wilkes	
Withers	
Trueax	
Boman	
Sim Vinton	
John Landon	

People of Whitewater Township

Men	Wives
Frank Hawley	
Hiram Noteware	
Edward (Ted) Cox	Millie
Horace K. Beecham	Lucy (Gurnee)
George Selkirk	Jeanette (Robertson)
Dan B. Scofield	Cordelia
Charles Truemain Scofield	Laura
Samuel Seeley	Martha (Depew)
Dr. Springstein	
Lafe Rickerd	
John Rickerd	
Len Rickerd	
William Merrill	
John Hamilton	Margaret (Bell)
Upsell Harrison	Rebecca (Copeland)
Mahlon Hoard	
Timothy Conant	
A. W. Eaton	
William Crisp	
Vet Cross	
Joel Cross	
George Broomhead	
Patrick Boyd	
James Boyd	
Hugh Boyd	
John Boyd	
Lonson Brown	
Edgar Pray	Mary (Broomhead)
Andrew Pray	Carrie (Estes)
Ed McCune	
Ed Hogeland	

People who lived around Mabel, Whitewater Township 100 years ago

The Samels and Watson families came together in 1855. Gervas Watson, Sr. came with his three sons, Fielding (Benny), William, Gervas, Jr., and his daughter Miriam, wife of William Samels. William and Miriam had a daughter Mary born in Bruce Mines, Ontario, Canada in 1854, four sons, Philip, Henery, Frank and William Jr., born close to what was later Mabel. Frank Samels married Mary Laubscher, and William Samels, Jr. married Bertha Seeley.

Antoine Linderleaf and wife Mary (Samels)
Three sons: Mones or Monze, Engle, and Edward
One daughter: Miriam

Gervas Watson's sons were
Fielding (Benny) and wife Sarah Lamson
William and wife Sarah
Gervas, Jr. and wife Anne Hamilton

Fielding (Benny) Watson and Sarah Lamson
Had three sons:
Walter and wife Maggie Thompson, who had one daughter, Dot Watson
James and wife Helen Pray
Hammond and wife Hortense Kocher
Three daughters:
Rose and husband Ed Glendenning
Rebecca, first husband William Pray, second husband Ed Pray
Charlotte, husband Ora Brown

Gervas Watson, Jr. and wife Annie Hamilton had four sons, Claude, George, William and Ben. Claude married Maude Gibbs, and Ben married Mabelle Corey.
and one daughter, Belle, who married Solomon Scott.

People of Whitewater Township

Figure 1.25: Benny Watson's 73rd Birthday, May 31, 1903
Back row: Hammond and Hortense Watson, Edward and Rose Ann Glendenning, Margaret and Walter Watson, Charles and Rebecca Pray, Helen and James Watson with baby John.

Front row: Mabel Glendenning, Sarah and Fielding (Benny) Watson, Charlotte Watson, Dorothy Watson, Austin Pray, Ada Watson, and Hobart Pray, sitting on the ground.

Courtesy of Carl Goss

People of Whitewater Township

Other settlers near Mabel were

Adolf Kaiser who married Miriam Samels after her first husband William Samels died in 1871.

George Humphrey, related to the Buttons

Ambrose Button and wife
His family was
James Button, first wife Edith, second wife Win
Charley, wife Berth
Frank, Earl, Harry, another one who died young.
He had three daughters Em, Mate, Jo Ann Button.

A man whose last name was Lawrence and wife Polly.

A.K. Fairbanks and first wife Mary (Thompson), second wife Emeline (Eastman)
His son Andrew and wife Sarah Broomhead
They had sons Clarence and Ora.

William Fairbanks and wife

Dell Fairbanks and wife Doan Broomhead

Columbia Boismier and wife
Five sons Art, Laun, William, Abb, and Urb
Two daughters Rose and Alice

Byron Hoyt and wife
Two sons Lute and Ross
Two daughters Hattie and Anne. Hattie married Engle Linderleaf.

Brown, Art

Richard Brown and wife Nellie Vinton had six sons:
Fred, Carl, Ora, Howard, Paul and Blyth. Howard married Agnes, and Paul married Hazel.

James Hammond and wife Mildred
They had five sons named James, Ed, Charley, Albert, and Godfrey D., who married Mary Cox

Edgar Pray, called Big Ed, and wife Mary Broomhead
Two sons:
Gilbert Pray and wife Effey
Orly and wife Emma Stites

Richard Pray and wife Melinda
Had five sons: Larry, Warren, Oliver, Thomas, and one son who died young. Thomas married Rose. They had one daughter

Steve Pray and wife
Had three sons:
George Pray, married Minnie
William Pray, married Rebecca Watson
Edgar Pray, called Little Ed, married Rebecca Watson after William's death
One daughter, Helen Pray who married James Watson

Andrew Pray and wife Carrie Estes
Had six sons: William, Clint, Cliff, Hazen, Mort, Ashley
and four daughters: Cora, Ethel, Gladys, Carrie. Cora married Grover Hammond

Weston Worden and wife Sarah J.
Had two sons: Loren, who married Hattie, and Ralph, who married Agnes
Three daughters: Mattie, Bertie and Lulla. Mattie married William Copeland.

Almond Young and wife Emily
Two sons: Alvie, Bert
One daughter: Dora, who married Neil Buller

Figure 1.26: Weston and Sarah Jane Worden, 1908
Courtesy of Kim Acker

Garnet Buller and wife

Others near Mabel were

Len Rickerd
Clements
Joel Cross
Vet Cross
William R. Durga
Ed McCune
Hattie Glendenning
Carl or Kirt Hasting

People of Whitewater Township

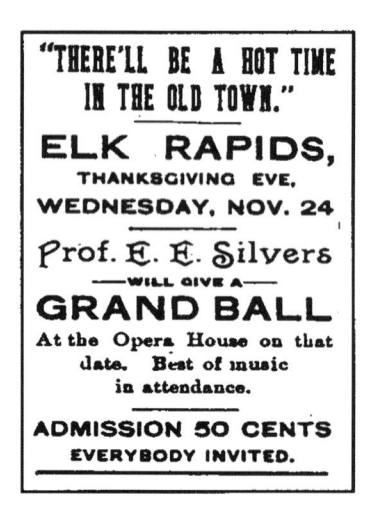

Figure 1.27: Elk Rapids Progess Advertisements, December 1888
Courtesy of Glenn Neumann

The Silvers Family

Dick Silver came to Williamsburg and lived sometime in the 1870's and early 1880's. He had five sons, G. Lote, Bert, Glen, Harry and Jim. They were show people. They were well known in vaudeville. They were called the Swiss Bell Ringers. Bert was born in 1860. When he was five years old he rang the bells in his father's act. When they came to Williamsburg, they lived here in the winter and went on the road with their show in the summer. They had a big two story house on Church St. They would put on shows in the upstairs. They later moved over to Acme.

G. Lote Silver later ran the Dreamland Theater in Traverse City. G. Lote Silver was widely known as the originator of old illustrated songs popular in the early days of the Cinema.

Bert Silver organized what was believed to be the first motorized circus with headquarters first at Standish and later at Crystal Lake near Standish. In 1909 he opened a theater in Greenville which he ran 'til 1939 when he sold it to Butterfield. He helped to organize and run the Greenville free fair. He was elected four times Mayor of Greenville.

Glen Silver ran a theater in Elk Rapids.

Entertainment

For pleasure, the early settlers would have neighborhood dances. They would go to one farmhouse one week. The next week or two they would go to another farmhouse. Empire Stites would play the fiddle or violin for them to dance by. He was quite particular to them as to keep step to his tune. Loren Worden was another man who would play the fiddle for them to dance by.

Sometimes when somebody had a birthday, they would have a party for them and present them with a chair or something.

People of Whitewater Township

Figure 1.28: Sarah Lamson Watson beside her cabin

Courtesy of Samels Collection

The Women of Whitewater Township

While I have the names of many of the men of the early settlers, I am sorry I do not have many of the names of the wives of these early settlers. The opening and clearing of this country would not have been possible without the hard work of the women along with the men, not only in the homes raising a family but out in the fields as the work in the early days had to be done by hand in the houses as well as the fields. They had to cook good substantial meals to sustain them and the men in their work and these women were good at preparing meals. Besides this there was the raising of children.

All the washing had to be done by hand, as well as the baking. There was no running to the store for baked goods. The butter was churned and worked by hand. The more butter was worked to get the water out of it, the better the butter was. The residue from the cream was called buttermilk which they used in baking. At first they had a stone jar with a wooden dasher they put the cream in and worked this dasher up and down to get the butter from the cream. Later, the barrel churn was invented which consisted of a wooden barrel set in a stand with a crank on the side and a lid that was screwed on tight. They put the cream in this barrel and turned the crank to separate the butter from the cream. This made it much easier.

Bread also had to be made and baked at home. Some women also spun their own wool from their sheep into yarn on a spinning wheel and knitted the yarn into socks and mittens and sweaters. They also bought cloth and made their own clothes for themselves and the whole family. Some even braided or wove their own rugs from carpet rags from clothes that had worn out. Some braided and sewed these rags together, and some wove them on a loom.

Some made their own soap. They would put ashes in a barrel, then pour water on them and when it drained out the bottom of the barrel, it would wash the lye from the ashes. This lye they would mix with scraps of fat to make soap. They could make either hard or soft soap.

Figure 1.29: Dr. William Holdsworth's Office, Williamsburg
Courtesy of Grand Traverse Pioneer and Historical Society

Doctors of Williamsburg

The first doctor of Williamsburg I have record of was a doctor named W. L. Springstein in the 1870's.

In the 1880's there was Dr. John White. He died in the mid 1880's. He was known as old Dr. White, but he was only 36 years old when he died. His son Ralph told me this.

Dr. Zina Pitcher from Kalkaska took over Dr. White's office after his death in 1885. In early 1886 Dr. Pitcher took a job as a surgeon in a marine hospital in Alaska.

Dr. Babcock of Kalkaska in early 1886 took over the office of Dr. Pitcher, formerly Dr. John White's practice in Williamsburg.

Other doctors were: Dr. Clark, Dr. Frank Holsworth, who worked with Dr. Clark, Dr. Vansickle, Dr. Gauntlett, and Dr. C. W. Bunce, assisted by his son Earl Bunce.

There was mention of a Dr. Ellis and a Dr. Ehle treating people around Williamsburg in 1885. Whether they lived here I do not know.

In 1921 a young doctor came to Williamsburg and stayed a short time, two or three months. I do not recall his name. There may have been other doctors I do not have a record of.

Dr. Bunce was the last permanent doctor in Williamsburg. I don't know when he came, but it was sometime before 1907 and he was here yet in 1918. He left in 1918 or 1919. His son Earl had left and had a practice downstate. He went down there with him, I believe. Dr. Bunce lived and had his office and kind of a drugstore on Church Street. In the teens he moved some of these buildings from here up to the new town on the north side of the road across from the post office, including a house and barn. Then his wife died so he did not do any more. He left soon after.

Diphtheria

Diphtheria

Williamsburg had its share of grief. In the fall of 1877 and winter of 1878 there was an outbreak of diphtheria. A news item of March 20, 1878 states it was still raging with several deaths in the preceding two weeks. One family by the name of Cross lost two kids in one night. They took them out and buried them in the night to lessen the danger of spreading the disease.

I do not know how many died from it, but one figure I heard was 25 or 30.

Father was nine years old at the time of this outbreak of diphtheria. One of the neighbor women, a Mrs. Brown, made sacks filled with camphor gum and asofetty and hung them around the kids necks to prevent them from getting it. Father could well remember the smell of the gum and asofetty. Father's family did not catch it, however.

Again in the fall of 1895 there was another outbreak of diphtheria which lasted through the winter of 1896. Several more died from it. They fenced the road off at the Creamery Hill on the east and Mc-Manaman hill on the west and did not let anybody in or out all winter.

Figure 1.30: Elk Rapids Progress advertisement, 1896

Courtesy of Glenn Neumann

Cemeteries

Some time before 1871 what is called the Old Cemetery at Williamsburg was established. This is the one on the south side of old M-72, east of the fire hall.

When they got the plot of ground they had a bee to clean it up. Everybody went and worked and took a lot for pay. Some of the early settlers who had been buried in the fields near their cabins were taken up and reburied here after the cemetery was established.

In the 1890's the Vintons started a new cemetery called Circle Hill because it was built on a round hill. This cemetery is located on the southern end of the Vinton Road. They moved some of the bodies from the old cemetery to the new cemetery, but did not plan to move those who had died from the diphtheria. Whether or not this is how the second epidemic of diphtheria got started, it could have been.

There was some scarlet fever at one time and some small pox at another time.

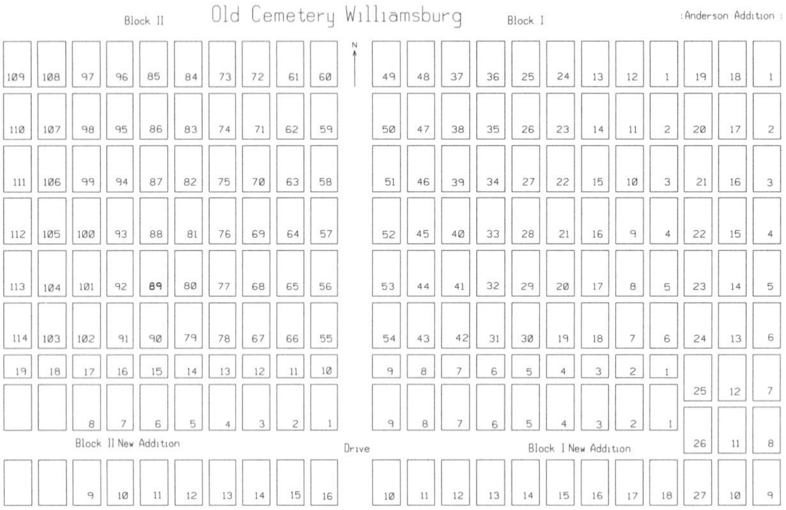

Cemeteries

Figure 1.31: Old Williamsburg Cemetery

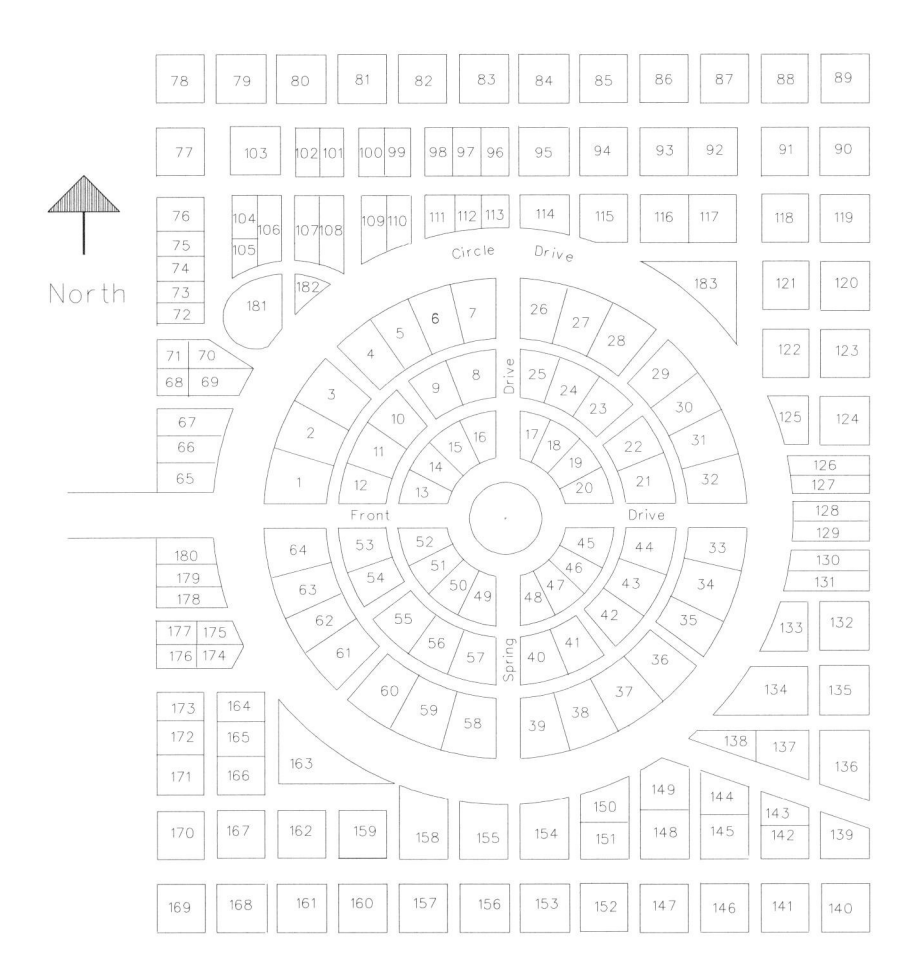

Figure 1.32: Circle Hill Cemetery, Williamsburg

Cemeteries

Figure 1.33: Williamsburg
Courtesy of Kathi Waggoner Gober

Figure 1.34: View of Williamsburg
Courtesy of Kathi Waggoner Gober

Williamsburg

Old Williamsburg

Church Street, according to the 1881 Atlas of Grand Traverse County, was the main business place at that time. On the south side of Church Street from the west going east was the Scofield grist mill on the west side of the creek near the pond. The sawmill was on the east side of the creek near the pond. Next was Stites shop, Carpenter's drug store, Scofield and son's house, Scofield Hotel and another C. T. Scofield house near the Vinton Road.

On the north side of Church Street the Methodist Church was built in 1881 on the west end of Church Street. Going east was the C. T. Scofield and Sons store. Next to this was the Dick Silvers house.

On the east side of Vinton Road from the south going north near the east end of Church Street was a blacksmith shop owned, I believe, by Mahlon Hoard, perhaps later by Oscar Marsh. I believe there was a barber shop along here, too. The Vinton store was started by Dave Vinton, Jr. and son Frank Vinton in about 1871. It was a general store of groceries, dry goods and some clothing, also boots and shoes and general merchandise. There was a lean-to on the side used for a drug store. Vinton also built a large house which I believe was used as a hotel. It later housed the Bell Telephone exchange, which Frank Vinton and his wife Emma took care of from the time the telephone wires came to Williamsburg in 1886 'til the death of both of them in 1930. Farther north was a hardware store owned by Charley Wills and son Hugh.

On the west side of Vinton Road at the corner of Vinton Road and Church Street was the White's house and store. This was a general store of groceries, dry goods, and some clothing. Dr. John White was one of the early doctors of Williamsburg. He died young leaving his wife with a family. In order to support the family, Mrs. White started the store with her son Ralph as manager. They later moved the business up to the new business district on Old M-72 near the Depot.

Williamsburg

Figure 1.35: Hugo Wills Store (originally Vinton's, second Ennest's)
Courtesy of Kathi Waggoner Gober

Going north on the west side of Vinton Road from the White's store at a later date was the Odd Fellows Hall, the Town Hall built in 1889, and a feed mill built by a man named Aslett. On the corner of Vinton Road and Old M-72 on the east side of Vinton Road and south side of old M-72 at, I believe, a later date a creamery was built. This was called Creamery Corners and the hill going east on old M-72 was called Creamery Hill.

The Vinton store was run by Dave Vinton and son Frank from 1871 'til sometime in the mid 1890's when it was sold to Albert Devries along with the sawmill. Devries did not want to run the store so he sold it to a man named James Ennest. Ennest ran it for quite a few years when he sold it to another party. About this time the store burnt down. Some of the township record books were believed to have burnt in this fire, as either the Township Supervisor or Clerk had a kind of office in this building.

The first telephone wires came to Acme in 1884 from Traverse City and on to Williamsburg in September of 1886.

Figure 1.36: White's Store at Church and Vinton
Courtesy of Karon Anderson

The Methodist Church was built in 1881. In 1882 money was raised by donations to buy the bell for the church.

In 1884 Leroy Randolph, 20 years old of Williamsburg, drowned in a lake south of here. The lake was called Randolph Lake after that. The Williamsburg people were having a picnic at the time.

In 1930 Eldon Samels drowned in the same lake.

In the 1880's a man by the name of S. W. Perkins manufactured mince meat around Williamsburg and sold it in the community, and some outside as far away as Cadillac.

Williamsburg

Figure 1.37: Charles Wills' Hardware Store, 1908
Courtesy of Kathi Waggoner Gober

Figure 1.38: Stores in New Town, c. 1921
Left to Right: Williamsburg Bank, Hobbs Store, Ralph White's Grocery. Nearest vehicle was Chance Seeley's 1923 Buick Roadster.
Courtesy of Lila Wilkinson

New Town

After the turn of the century, the stores began moving up nearer the Depot on Old M-72.

Gilbert Pray built a potato warehouse in 1912 and later a grain elevator.

Upsel Hobbs built a general store of groceries, dry goods, clothing, hardware, drugs, and some farm machinery. You could buy almost anything here you could in Traverse City. He ran this store 'til 1921 when he died. Mrs. Hobbs then ran it with Alfred Johnson as Manager 'til about 1927 when she was killed in an automobile accident. It ran a year or so, and was then turned into strictly a grocery store by the son Charley Hobbs. Later it was moved into the old Bank building and run by other people 'til Howard Brown took it over sometime in the 1930's. It was run by him 'til he became ill, then by his daughter Doris Gay 'til she sold it. This store was run by Randy Stites in 1985.

On the west side of the Hobbs store another building was built by, I believe, Hugo Wills. Ralph White took over this building and moved his store up here sometime in the teens. He ran it 'til 1928, then turned it over to Lute Hoyt who ran it 'til 1943, then closed it out.

Daymon Seeley then ran a store at his place on the north side of Old M-72 for a few years. This was a grocery store. He also sold hardware here for a few years.

Sometime in the teens, Power, Whitmore and Power built a bank to the east of the Hobbs store. They ran it for about ten years, then closed it out in 1929, paying off the depositors in full.

Daymon Seeley built the first garage to repair automobiles in Williamsburg some time in the teens. He ran it for many years. Then his son Evert ran it 'til it was closed.

Clint Drake, Earl Gay and Ken Watson also had repair garages in Williamsburg in the 1920's, 30's, 40's, 50's and 60's.

Williamsburg

Phil Omen had a blacksmith shop here on the north side of Old M-72 in the early 1920's. In the winter of 1923 Ralph Worden ran this shop for the winter. This was the last blacksmith shop in Williamsburg.

Sometime in the teens, Robert Clow ran a store of mostly groceries on the north side of Old M-72. This building was later owned by Charley Shaw. Later Krogel's owned the building and Mrs. Krogel ran a grocery store here for awhile.

Sumner Gaines had a barber shop in the north side of Old M-72 in the teens and 1920's. Then Frank Bartlett ran the shop for awhile. It then burnt down. This was the last barber shop in Williamsburg.

These stores and shops and Seeley's garage lay to the west of the Hobbs and Whites stores on the north side of the road across from the Depot, which was on the south side of the road. The Hobbs and White stores were on the south side of the road.

Between the Hobb and White stores and the Depot on the south side of the road, the R. C. M. Gardner family lived. He drilled water wells. Mrs. Gardner had an ice cream parlor in her home for a few years. Wayne Wilkinson married the Gardner's daughter and carried on the well drilling for several years 'til his death in 1968.

The Depot has been torn down. The Hobbs store was turned into a gym for the school in the 1930's. The White's store building and the old Bank building (now Stites store) still stand near the Post Office.

Another building called the bee hive, that had several rooms in it to rent to people to live in, was located on the north side of Old M-72 across from the Hobbs and White stores. Across from the Post Office were the buildings Dr. Bunce moved up from Church Street in the teens.

This was known as the new town. In the mid 1960's the state relocated the road M-72 which cuts through the heart of the old town and leaves the new town on a side street.

Schools

Early schools of the present Township of Whitewater from the reprint of the History of the Grand Traverse region of 1884:

No. 1, known as the Webster or Broomhead School in Section 10 Town 27 North Range 9 West on the west side of Broomhead Road two miles south of the north town line of Town 27 North Range 9 West.

No. 2, Old log school built before 1881 in Section 36, Town 28 North Range 9 West on the east side of the Skegemog Road near the south end. It was replaced by two schools in 1881, one later called the North Mabel School on the northeast corner of Section 35 Town 28 North Range 9 West on the west side of the Skegemog Road and south side of the Lossie Road. The other was called the South Mabel School located on the Deal Road.

No. 3, called the Elk Lake School located in Section 4 Town 28 Range 9 West on the west side of Elk Lake Road near south line of Section 4.

No. 4, Williamsburg School located in Section 4 Town 27 North Range 9 West on the west side of what is now called the Williamsburg Road approximately 100 rods south of the north township line of Town 27.

No. 5, known as the Bloodgood School in Section 22 Town 28 North Range 9 West on the east side of what is now called the Cram Road.

In 1862 James O. Bloodgood came to Whitewater Township. Some time after this he built the first school in Williamsburg located in, I believe, Section 33 Town 28 North Range 9 West, and installed Miss Sarah Spencer as teacher.

This school was later replaced by the school No. 4 located in Section 4 Town 27 North Range 9 West. Some time after 1884 another school called the Lyons School was built southwest of Williamsburg, just where I do not know.

Schools

These schools were one room schools up through the 8th grade, except the No. 4 school in Williamsburg which was a 10th grade school in later years. Just when they started the 10th grade I do not know.

These schools ran 'til 1920 or 21 when the South Mabel, the Webster or Broomhead, the Lyons and Bloodgood Schools consolidated with the Williamsburg school and formed a Kindergarten through 12th grade school and built a schoolhouse in Section 33 Town 28 on the west side of Elk Lake Road.

The North Mabel School ran as an 8th grade school 'til 1941 or 42 when they transported the kids to Williamsburg and eventually consolidated with Williamsburg.

The Elk Lake School ran for several years. Then they transported the kids to Elk Rapids and eventually consolidated with Elk Rapids schools.

The Williamsburg School ran 'til 1958 when the people voted to consolidate with the Elk Rapids Schools, making Whitewater Township almost all consolidated with the Elk Rapids Schools.

A little bit of the southwest corner of Whitewater Township is in the East Bay or Traverse City school district.

See bibliography: [1, The Traverse Region Historical and Descriptive]

Road Building and Maintenance in Whitewater Township

In the early days instead of levying a tax of money to maintain the roads, the settlers were assessed so much time to be spent on the road, some a half day, some a full day, some more according to how much property they owned. If a farmer would buy a wide tire wagon instead of a narrow tire, he would be allowed some on his time as a wide tire would pack the road bed down more than a narrow tire.

What was called a Highway Road Commissioner was elected by the people on their annual Election Day on the first Monday after the first Tuesday in April. They would also elect a Road Overseer to help the Highway Commissioner.

They also had what was a Pathmaster system. A Pathmaster was a man appointed one for each road or two. His job was to take the landowners out and have them work their assessed time on the road. He had a roll with the names of the owners of property on each road and how much time they were assessed. Each Pathmaster would have one or two roads and crossroads to look after. This work was done by hand or by teams of horses with scrapers.

My father, Frank Samels, was Pathmaster of the Skegemog Road one year in 1896.

The Pathmaster system was done away with a long time ago. They went to levying taxes for roads and the Highway Commissioner then hired men and teams to maintain the roads. In the 1930's the roads were all turned over to the County to maintain. My Uncle William Samels was Highway Commissioner of Whitewater Township for several years.

Road Building and Maintenance

Figure 1.39: Drake's Garage, Williamsburg
Earl Gay, Richard Dean, and Clinton Drake
Courtesy of Doris Gay

Garages of Williamsburg

Daymon Seeley built the first garage to repair automobiles in Williamsburg sometime in the teens before 1920. He ran it for many years. Then his son Evert ran it 'til it was closed. He built a new building to the west of the old building which Evert used to do his garage work. In the last few years he did auto repair work. He built this building about 1946.

Daymon Seeley and his wife Lucy then ran a hardware and grocery store in the old building for a few years.

These buildings are across from where the Depot sat on the north side of Old M-72. Clinton Drake took over the Mennonite Church building which was built at an earlier time and used as a church for awhile. They did not have enough members to keep it going so Clinton Drake bought it and made a garage out of it in the later 1920's. He ran it for several years, repairing automobiles. He remodeled it making a lower building out of it. This building is on the north side of Old M-72 a little way west of the Elk Lake Road. When he got through running it, he leased or sold it to other parties.

The other parties who ran a repair garage for autos in it were W. Hannah for awhile, Aubrey Carmien, Earl Gay, and last Kenneth Watson bought it and ran it for several years. In 1955 Kenneth Watson built a large addition to it on the west side.

Earl Gay built an auto repair garage on the southwest corner of Old M-72 and Williamsburg Road in the 1940's, which he ran for several years. Then Louis Vert ran it for awhile.

William Stites and his sons also ran a repair garage here for awhile. It is idle now.

There was no auto repair garage in Williamsburg in 1986.

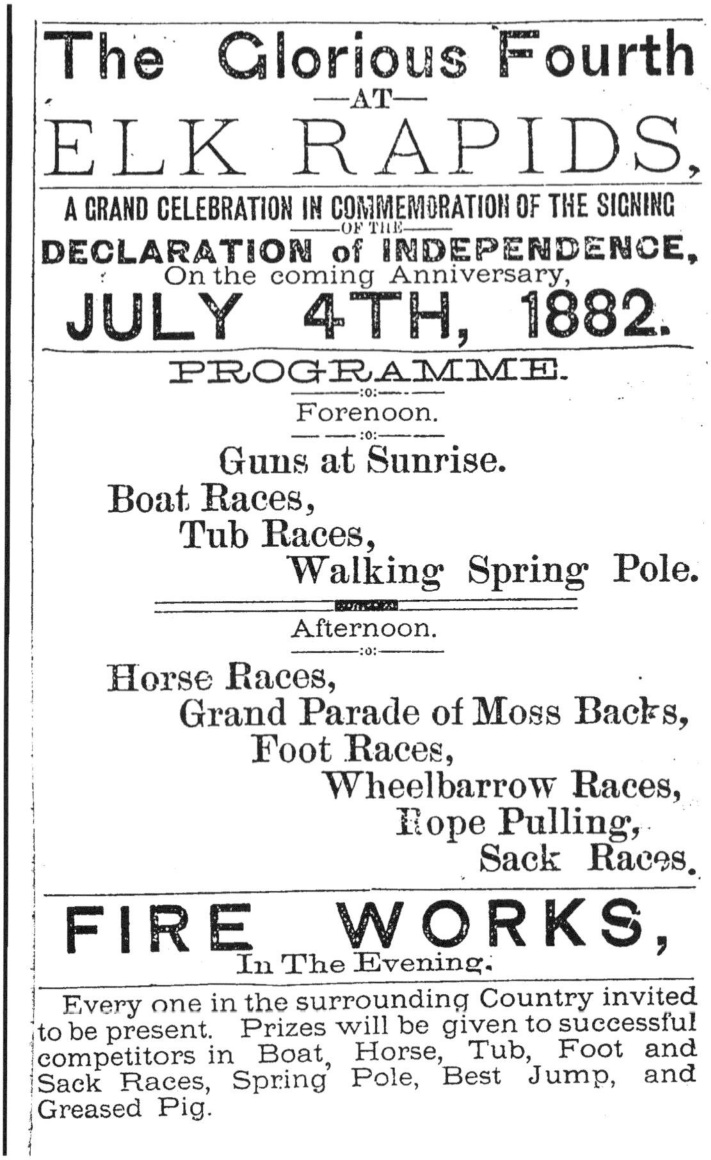

Garages of Williamsburg

The Glorious Fourth
—AT—
ELK RAPIDS,
A GRAND CELEBRATION IN COMMEMORATION OF THE SIGNING
—OF THE—
DECLARATION of INDEPENDENCE,
On the coming Anniversary,
JULY 4TH, 1882.

PROGRAMME.

Forenoon.

Guns at Sunrise.
Boat Races,
  Tub Races,
    Walking Spring Pole.

Afternoon.

Horse Races,
  Grand Parade of Moss Backs,
    Foot Races,
      Wheelbarrow Races,
        Rope Pulling,
          Sack Races.

FIRE WORKS,
In The Evening.

Every one in the surrounding Country invited to be present. Prizes will be given to successful competitors in Boat, Horse, Tub, Foot and Sack Races, Spring Pole, Best Jump, and Greased Pig.

Figure 1.40: 1882 Elk Rapids newspaper advertisement
Courtesy of Glenn Neummann

Township Officers

In addition to electing a Highway Commissioner and Road Overseer at the annual election, a Township Supervisor, a Township Clerk, a Township Treasurer, one or two Justices of the Peace and a Constable were elected.

The Township Supervisor went around once a year, usually in May, to assess the value of the property in the Township. He also assessed the personal property. You were allowed so much personal property; over that amount you were taxed for it. The Supervisor had to call at each residence in the Township to make these assessments.

The Supervisors also attended the County Board of Supervisors, which met about once a month to handle the affairs of the County. This board was made up of one Supervisor from each Township in the County. It has been changed to a County Board of Commissioners based on the population. Thus Whitewater and Acme Townships only have one representative, where before they had two, one for each township.

The Township Clerk kept the records for the Township.

The Township Treasurer collected the taxes for the Township.

The Justices of the Peace acted as judges in the Township.

The Constable acted as a police officer in the Township.

The Supervisor, Clerk, Treasurer and Justices of the Peace made up the Township Board, which handled the affairs of the Township. These officers of the Township were elected for a term of one year at a time. This election was held the first Monday after the first Tuesday in April every year. Later the law was changed so they were elected for two years at a time. Now they are elected for four year terms in the fall.

At these election days, they would have the polls open all day for the people to vote by ballot. Some state and county officers were elected on this day also. On these election days they would close the polls for one hour in the afternoons to hold what was called a town meeting when the residents of the township would vote by acclamation or voice vote to raise money to maintain the roads and other matters pertaining to the Township.

Later the courts said this was not legal as the polls were by law to be kept open all day, so the state made a law that they would have to hold their annual town meeting the Saturday before the election day.

Now the spring election has been done away with and all the officers, Township, County, State and Nation, are elected in the fall.

Mabel

Mabel was a little town east of Williamsburg, established about 1892 when the Chicago and West Michigan Railroad came through. It was named Mabel after Mabel Bates, a daughter of Thomas T. Bates, who was a Traverse City publisher.

A man by the name of Carl Hasting came up from Grand Rapids and set up a steam powered sawmill here. I am not sure but I believe that was around the time the railroad came through in 1892. There was a little store here and also a Post Office here for a few years. Byron Hoyt set up a shingle mill here, employing six or seven men. He also ran a store and took care of the Post Office.

There was a siding on the railroad where the settlers loaded logs and cordwood on the railroad to go to Elk Rapids. The farmers also loaded potatoes on the railroad here. Later, Gilbert Pray ran the store and also had a meat wagon peddling meat around the community. In 1908 he hired Gardner and his son, well drillers in the community, to drill a well on the property. They struck an artesian flow which was believed to be the strongest flowing well in the state. It shot 45 feet in the air. This well is still flowing here, although the town of Mabel is but a memory.

A Post Office was established at Mabel on August 15, 1892. Albert Fairbanks was the first Postmaster. Andrew Pray was named Postmaster in 1912, serving until the Post Office closed in 1918.

In 1910 there was a train wreck on the railroad east of Mabel where the railroad crossed the Skegemog Road. A miscalculation in the timing let the stone run from Petoskey come head-on with a freight train. The two engines telescoped and Walter Beeman, the brakeman from Elk Rapids, was killed. There was another train wreck around Mabel but I do not have the particulars on it so I cannot write about it. It seems from what I heard a log rolled off from a logging train going through Mabel and struck the switch on a side track. It opened the switch so the train continued on down the main track and some of the cars went on the side track.

Mabel

Courtesy of Kathi Waggoner Gober

Figure 1.41: 1910 Mabel Train Wreck
Courtesy of Karon Anderson

Baggs Road

Some time before 1885 the Dexter and Noble Company of Elk Rapids built a store on the north end of Baggs Road on Round Lake. Mr. James Evarett ran it. Any supplies not available at the store could be got from Elk Rapids. James Evarett closed this store in 1885 and opened a store in Barker Creek. The company then moved the building to Elk Rapids. They loaded it on one of their scows that they used to haul wood down the lakes for their furnace to smelt iron. They towed the building down the lakes. It still stands there off Dexter Street behind the building where Joe's Antiques Store was.

The first settlers on the north end of Baggs Road on Round Lake were named Sutherland. When they got old, Mrs. Sutherland had a son by the name of John Smith who came here from Australia to take care of them. He married Millie Eisler whose parents lived on the south end of the Baggs Road. The Sutherlands died and John Smith died. Then Millie Smith married George Baggs. They had one son, John Baggs.

Edward and Millie Cox bought the next property south of there on the west side of the road in 1871. They had a son and daughter, Upsell and Mary Cox.

Upsell Harrison, a half brother of Edward Cox, got the next property south of Coxes. His wife was a sister of William Copeland, Sr. They had two daughters, Mary and Emma. Emma Harrison married Frank Vinton.

William Copeland, Sr., the first settler in Kalkaska County, settled there in 1855 on the east side of Baggs Road on the north side of now M-72. He married Mary Swaney. They had four sons and a daughter who grew to adulthood. Their names were William, Jr., Edgar, Thomas, Henry and Rose. Rose Copeland married Dennis Hoxsie.

Gervas Watson, Sr. came in September of 1855 and bought 160 acres of land along the south side of what is now M-72 between the Baggs and Skegemog Roads. He was a widower, his wife having died

Baggs Road

in England. He had four sons and a daughter. Their names were John, Fielding, William, Gervas, Jr. and Miriam. John didn't come down from Canada with the rest of his family. Gervas built a log house near where the present Ray Boyd house stands (1986). He lived here with his son William 'til his death in 1866. He gave the east 80 acres to his son William.

William Watson lived here 'til the fall of 1877 when he sold the land to Upsell Harrison and moved to Arkansas. The last summer William Watson lived here, 1877, he built the upright part of the house that still stands in 1986.

After William Watson moved away Hursh Hobbs, who married Mary Harrison, daughter of Upsell Harrison, lived here and farmed it in the latter part of the 1880's. They had a son and daughter named Upsell and Opel.

South of here on the west side of the Baggs Road Delany Hammond, who married Mary Cox, the daughter of Edward Cox, owned a piece of land where they lived. They had one daughter Cassie. Cassie Hammond married Philip Ray.

On the east side of the Baggs Road across from the Hammonds a party by the name of Eisler lived. He was Swiss, she was German. They were parents of Millie Smith Baggs.

Off the south end of Baggs Road a man by the name of Joe Place lived. After him on the same place Joe Mason, who married Lavina Pray, lived. Julian and Loree Schlagel also lived off the south end of Baggs Road.

Settlers on the Baggs Road from 1855 on until 1900

Quite a few of these people lived here after 1900. From the north going south:

    Mr. and Mrs. Sutherland
    John and Millie Smith. John Smith was Mrs. Sutherland's son
    George and Millie Smith Baggs. John Smith was Millie Smith Baggs' first husband.

Edward and Millie Cox	1871
Upsell and Fanny Cox	
Mr. and Mrs. Upsell Harrison	
William, Sr., and Mary Copeland	1855
William, Jr. and Maddie Copeland	
Edward and Cora Copeland	
Gervas Watson, Sr.	1855
William and Sarah Watson	1855
Hursh and Mary Hobbs	
Delany and Mary Cox Hammond	

    Jacob and Margaret Eisler, parents of Millie Smith Baggs.
    Joseph Place, off the south end of the Baggs Road, and later on the same farm lived
    Joe and Lavina Mason

On the Baggs Road after 1900, before 1950, and some after 1950; north going south:

    John and Florence Baggs
    Henry and Nora Cox
    Lewis and Amelia Cox
    Mr. and Mrs. Joe Cox
    Walter and Irene Cox
    Lawrence and Marjorie Copeland
    Richard and Ruby Copeland
    Philip and Cassie Hammond Ray
    Ray and Elaine Ray Boyd
    Lowell and Ladore Whiteford Ray
    Thomas and Alice Dockery
    William and Lurance Mason

Baggs Road

Some renters lived on the Baggs Road during the early 1900's. On the Vinton farm, formerly the Harrison farm, later the Lew Cox farm:

Mr. and Mrs. Houghton and family
Burdette and Olive Orcutt and family
Lyle and Osa Orcutt, along with Loren and Hattie Worden
Mr. and Mrs. Randel
There were some others, but I do not have the names.

On the Philip Ray farm lived a man by the name of Sawyer, and Mr. and Mrs. Robinson and perhaps others.

Early settlers on what is now M-72 between Skegemog and Baggs Road:

J.M. or J.B. Merrill, perhaps both on the east end, north side of the road at a very early date of 1858 or before. Later, H.S. Beach on this same place in 1869.

On the south side of the road,

Josiah Curtis in the 1870's and a party named Johnson in the 1890's.

Emily Young
Mr. and Mrs. Almond Young on the north side of the road near M-72 and Skegemog Roads in the 1800's. The Youngs had three children: Alvie, Bert and Dora, and they raised a girl named Rose who married Thomas Pray.
Neil and Dora Young Buller lived on the same place.
Garnet and Gladys Buller in the 1900's. They had three children: Neil, Eva and Garnet, Jr.
Edward and Cora Copeland on the south side of this road in the mid 1900's, and on the former Curtis farm. William and Lucille Copeland Warner lived on this place after the mid 1950's.
Warren Pray lived on the south side of this road in the first half of 1900.

On the Merrill farm there were many renters with such names as White, Hanson, Goodrich, and Stafford. A man named Aslett owned it for awhile and mostly rented it in the 1900's. J. R. Eiszner bought it and owned it for a few years, then sold it to Lewis and Amelia Cox.

On the Lossee Road at an early date a party named Wilkes, grandparents of Thomas Pray, lived at that location. This spelling may not be correct.

Truman and Julia Lossee lived on the Lossee Road in much of the first half of the 1900's.

Oliver Pray lived on the Lossee Road in much of the first half of the 1900's.

On the Section line between Sections 24 and 25, on the east side of the Skegemog Road a little over a hundred rods east of the road a party by the name of Withers lived here sometime before 1900. Again, this name may not be spelled correctly.

Steamer Ida's time table for season of 1888.

MORNING RUN.

Time of Leaving.	Time of Arriving.
East Port......6 00	Torch Lake...6.15
Torch Lake....6.20	Balls Landing.7.30
Ball's Landing.7.35	Clam River...7.50
Clam River....8.00	Spencer Creek.8.30
Spencer Creek.8.45	Torch River...9.30
Torch River...9.45	Elk Rapids...11.00

AFTERNOON RUN.

Leaving.	Arriving.
Elk Rapids....1.15	Torch River...2.45
Torch River...3.00	Spencer Creek.3.45
Spencer Creek.4.00	Clam River....4.30
Clam River....4.45	Ball's Landing.5.00
Ball's Landing.5.05	Torch Lake...6.00
Torch Lake...6.05	East Port.....6.20

The Ida has been nicely refitted for the accomodation of the traveling public and time will be as punctual as possible. This is the best way to go north from Elk Rapids as you can pass through the beautiful inland lakes. The Ida makes connection with the bay and lake boats.

Respectfully,
HAWLEY & SHARP,
Proprietors.

STEAMER

J. J. MORLEY

CAPT. J. H. McCLUSKY.

Morning Run.—Will leave Old Mission every morning at 6 o'clock, Elk Rapids 7; arrive at East Bay at 8:30, Traverse City 9 o'clock, in time for morning train.

Returning, Bus leaves all Hotels, Traverse City, at 7:30 A. M., arriving at East Bay at 8:30, Elk Rapids 10, Old Mission 10:30 o'clock.

Afternoon Run.—Leave Old Mission at 11 A. M., Elk Rapids 1 P. M., arrive at East Bay at 2:30, Traverse City at 3, in time for afternoon express train.

Returning, Bus leaves hotels, Traverse City, at 2:15, arrive at East Bay at 3, Elk Rapids 4:30, Old Mission 5 P. M.

Close connections made at Elk Rapids with the steamer "Ida" for Spencer Creek, Bellaire, Mancelona, Torch Lake and all points on the inland lakes.

July 16, 1888.

INLAND LAKE ROUTE.

STR. ODD.FELLOW.

CAPTAIN, JOS. HAWLEY

TIME TABLE.

GOING SOUTH, A. M.	GOING NORTH, P. M.
Leave Eastport......6 15	Leave Elk Rapids ...3 00
Torch Lake...7 00	Torch River...4 10
Clam River...8 15	Alden..........4 45
Alden..........9 10	Clam River...5 00
Torch River..9 45	Torch Lake...6 30
Arrive Elk Rapids..11 00	Arrive Eastport 7 00

Makes connections at Elk Rapids with trains going North and South, at Alden with all trains, and at Elk Rapids with all bay and lake steamers.

OLD MISSION--ELK RAPIDS ROUTE.

STR. ONEKAMA

J. U. EMORY, MASTER.

FORENOON RUN.

Leave Old Mission at 8, arrive Elk Rapids at 8:40; leave Elk Rapids at 10, arrive Old Mission at 10:40.

AFTERNOON RUN.

Leave Old Mission at 12 m., arrive Elk Rapids at 12:40; leave Elk Rapids at 3, arrive Old Mission at 3:40. Leave Old Mission at 5, arrive Elk Rapids at 5:40; leave Elk Rapids at 6, arrive Old Mission at 6:40.

Figure 1.42: 1888 and 1895 Boat Schedules
Courtesy of Glenn Neumann

Barker Creek

A history of Whitewater Township would not be complete without a mention of Barker Creek, a little town in the adjoining Township of Clearwater in Kalkaska County.

What hamlet so small in the lumbering days could boast of three churches and no saloons? It must have been a community of the purest people. In addition to three churches, there were two stores, a band hall also called Opera House, a Depot, Post Office located in one of the stores, a school house, potato warehouse, sawmills, a shingle mill, and a cemetery.

There was the Methodist Church on a lot off the Copeland farm on the north side of what is now M-72 a ways east of the Baggs Road. A little farther east was the schoolhouse, also on a lot off the Copeland farm on the north side of the road. A Church of Christ was built on the corner of M-72 and Dockery Road. I believe there was a store near these corners at first. A party named Stover had a house here also on the north side of the road near the schoolhouse.

The business then moved farther east where James Evarett had a store on the north side of the road. Before 1885 Mr. Evarett ran a store on the north end of the Baggs Road on Round Lake for the Dexter and Noble Company of Elk Rapids. He closed this store in 1885 and opened his store in Barker Creek in 1885 which he ran for several years.

Western Union opened a telegraph office here in 1885 with James Evarett as manager. The Chicago and West Michigan Railroad came through here in 1892 and built a Depot behind the Evaretts store. This Depot burnt in 1906. Cox built a potato warehouse near the Depot. A little farther east on the north side of the road was a Band Hall.

On the south side of the road, now M-72, across from the Evaretts store, William Hewitt and Martin Moran built a store. Mr. Moran ran this store as long as he was able. Then John Brennaman ran it 'til his death in 1934. A little farther east on the south side of the road was the Catholic Church and cemetery. This church was completed in 1883 and discontinued in 1946.

The Church of Christ was hit by lightening and burnt down. The Methodist Church was torn down. The Catholic Church was moved to Kalkaska.

William Copeland, Sr., had a sawmill here. He was a millwright and built his own sawmill and thrashing machine. He also helped to build mills for other people around the country, including Hannah and Lay of Traverse City. Myron Stover's father had a sawmill at Barker Creek at an early date. I believe there were other sawmills there.

Byron Hoyt had a shingle mill here for awhile, I believe in the later 1890's.

Before the Post Office was established in 1874, mail was carried by an Indian named Philip Post from Acme through Barker Creek and on up north.

The Post Office was established in 1874 with William H. Bockes as first Postmaster. The mail came from Acme on a stage once a week. In the 1880's it was extended to twice a week. In the later 1880's, the mail was carried three times a week by stage from Acme to Barker Creek 'til the railroad came through in 1892. Then it was carried on the train.

The Post Office was housed in the stores and perhaps in some of the homes, according to who was Postmaster. There were several Postmasters from the time the Post Office was established in 1874 'til it was abandoned in 1937. Rolly Champney was the last Postmaster.

Barker Creek was named for the Creek that ran through it. A dam was built on the creek but was never used.

Old Settlers of Barker Creek

Figure 1.43: Barker Creek Lumber Camp
Courtesy of Lynda VanAmburg

William Copeland, Sr., the first settler in Kalkaska County, came in 1855 and settled on the northeast corner of Baggs Road and now M-72 a ways west of the site of Barker Creek. He was the only settler east of the County line for several years. Myron Stover's father had a sawmill at Barker Creek at an early date.

William H. Bockes settled here in 1866.
Mr. Moran in the fall of 1869.
Other settlers were
William Hewitt
Peter Desmond
Chaney Family
J. Steve
John Mason
Cornelius Cronin in 1869
John H. Letherby in 1866

Old Settlers of Barker Creek

These settlers settled within a two or three mile radius of Barker Creek.

Up south of Barker Creek in Wilson Township south of Clearwater were many Irish settlers. It was called up in Ireland. While all of these may not have been Irish, many of them were, some having come from Ireland. Their names:

Patrick Dockery
Donahue
Dempsey
Storms
L. A. Haynes in 1866
William Hough in 1866
William Gibson
Thomas Johnson

A few settlers farther east of Barker Creek were:

Name	Date	Location
Eli Gillett	1868	Section 22
A. T. Kellogg	1868	Section 14
Thomas Lancaster	1870 With parents	Section 26
Thomas Hunley	1869 With parents	Section 22
Richard Towers	1862	Section 22
D. P. Beebe	1867	Section 36
Norman Ross	1867	Section 36
Elisha W. Clement	1867	Section 14
A. C. Beebe	1868	Section 36

France or French Landing

North and east of Barker Creek, the Round Lake swamp was covered with dense cedar timber. It produced thousands of giant telegraph poles, cedar lumber by the trainloads and hardwood lumber in vast quantities.

A large amount of the property in this swamp was owned by a man named McNulty. He planned to make a game refuge of the property but he died and his plans did not materialize. A man by the name of Link Simmons next acquired the timber rights and set up a shingle mill, as the vast cedar in the swamp was ideal for making shingles. Next the French Lumber Company of Battle Creek came in to harvest the hardwood and pine on the McNulty property. This gave it the name of France or French Landing.

The Pere Marquette Railroad had a siding here to haul the lumber out. The French Lumber Company built a large steam powered sawmill here and cut a vast quantity of lumber daily. The saws in the mill were bandsaws.

They put down a strong artesian well to supply water for the boiler. This well was so strong you could not catch a cup of water for a drink by holding the cup directly under the stream. You had to hold the cup under the edge of the stream. John Warner, who I knew, ran the engine for this company. He said the water from this well had such a little lime in it, he did not have to clean the flues in the boiler.

The French Lumber Company left here when the timber was all cut sometime in the teens, 1917 or 1918, and moved to Lansing. John Warner went with them and worked for them down there.

The shingle mill gave work for about 25 men, and the sawmill for many more around the mill and harvesting the timber. The railroad siding was used for awhile after the mill left for shipping wood and railroad ties.

Figure 1.44: Winter Snows
Courtesy of Samels Collection

Figure 1.45: Winter at the Farm
Courtesy of Samels Collection

Ice Storm

In 1922 there was an ice storm that tied everything up for several days.

Around the 22nd of February 1922 it snowed all day, a fine sugary snow by night. There was 10 or 12 inches. Then it turned warm and rained on it. It then turned cold again and put about two inches of solid ice on top of the snow. It was great fun for us kids as there was almost skating on top of the snow. You could slide down hill anywhere.

But it tied up the railroads and the telephone wires were down. This storm reached from south of Kingsley to Petoskey. It was nine days before the trains could get through from Kingsley to Williamsburg. They had to hire men to go ahead of the snow plough on the railroads with axes and chop the ice so the plow could clear the tracks. We were nine days without mail.

The telephone wires were down. The only way they could get a message from Petoskey to Grand Rapids was around through Iowa and back to Grand Rapids.

The roads were not plowed for cars yet then, so all travel on the roads was by teams. But the ice made it difficult for teams of horses.

Ice Storm

Figure 1.46: Tugs Towing Cordwood
Courtesy of Elk Rapids Area Historical Society

Boats and Railroads

Could I have chosen another time to live in the past, I would have chosen the time when the boats were traveling the Chain of Lakes; Elk, Round, Torch, Clam and Lake Bellaire; and when the railroads were beginning to come into the country.

There were many boats traveling these lakes in the 1870's, 80's, 90's and the first decade of the 20th century, but especially in the 1880's. For nearly 40 years these boats traveled these lakes with such names as the Queen of the Lakes, the Ruth, the Mabel, the Ida, the Valley Queen, the Time, the Jennie Silkman, the Albatross (a paddle wheel tug), the Lizzie Rose, the Grass Goose, and the Maple Leaf. These boats traveled these lakes 'til the railroad made it unprofitable. They traveled from Elk Rapids to Eastport, Alden, Clam River, and Bellaire with stops in between, especially at Skegemog Point. You could board these boats at any of these towns and travel to any of the other towns on the lakes. You could board the boats at Skegemog Point and go to Elk Rapids for a quarter. The Mabel and the Ruth made regular stops at Skegemog Point. If any of the other boats stopped there, I do not know. Kings let them use his dock on Round Lake at the Point after he got there sometime in the 1890's. Before that I do not know if they could stop at Skegemog Point.

There were many boats on the Great Lakes and Bays. First were the sailboats, before and sometime after the steam engine was invented. The sailboats were the only means of travel on the Great Lakes for hundreds of years and for thousands of years on the oceans. But they were at the mercy of the winds. When the winds did not blow, they did not go. These boats hauled both passengers and freight. They hauled much lumber from the sawmills around the lakes to Chicago and other cities to the south.

Then the steam engine was invented to run the boats. They did not have to wait for the wind. First was the side wheeler with a paddle-wheel on each side of the boat. Then came the propellers, which were speedier and not so cumbersome as the side wheeler.

Boats and Railroads

There were many of these boats traveling the Great Lakes. Hannah and Lay Company of Traverse City had several boats on the Bays and Great Lakes. Dexter and Noble Company of Elk Rapids had boats on the Grand Traverse Bays and Great Lakes, and also on the Chain of Lakes.

There were also steamship lines running boats from Chicago to Buffalo and into Lake Superior.

The sailboats and steamboats were the only means of travel for hundreds and thousands of years. But they were limited to the waterways and the sailboats could not go when the wind did not blow.

The means of travel on the land was by ox team or horses. When the railroads came in, they replaced the oxen and horses for travel. They could go almost anywhere on the land and were not limited to the waterways like the boats were. It must have been a great feeling to the settlers when the railroads came in and they did not have to depend on oxen and horses for travel. The steam engine on the railroad was much faster and did not have to stop to rest.

The railroads first came into the area in the early 1870's to Kalkaska and Traverse City. For the next 40 years or so they built up to their peak before they started to decline.

There were six railroads serving the five county area of Grand Traverse, Kalkaska, Antrim, Benzie, and Leelanau Counties, with four serving Traverse City. They were the

1. Grand Rapids and Indiana (G R and I)
2. Chicago and West Michigan, taken over by the Pere Marquette, and later by the Chesapeake & Ohio.
3. Manistee & North Eastern
4. Traverse City, Leelanau & Manistique, with a car ferry between Northport and Manistique until 1906.
5. Empire & Southeastern
6. Toledo & Ann Arbor to Frankfort.

Boats and Railroads

The last two did not enter Traverse City.

The first railroad to enter the area was the Grand Rapids and Indiana which came through Kalkaska from the south with a spur into Traverse City from Walton Junction in 1872-73. In 1882 this railroad was extended from Petoskey to Mackinaw. You could get on this railroad at Kalkaska, Traverse City or any other town along the way and go north to Mackinaw and across the straits by ferry to the railroads in the Upper Peninsula, or you could go south and connect up with other railroads and go anywhere in the United States.

There were no other railroads in the area 'til 1890 when the Chicago and West Michigan came into Traverse City from the south. From that time on there were many railroads serving the five county area for the next 30 or 40 years.

In 1892 the Chicago and West Michigan came north from Traverse City through Acme, Bates, Williamsburg, Barker Creek with a spur into Elk Rapids from Williamsburg, and went on up north from Barker Creek through Rapid City, Alden (Spencer Creek, as it was called), and on to Bellaire and Central Lake in 1892, and on up to Petoskey in 1894. The little towns of Bates and Mabel were founded then in 1892. Bates was between Acme and Williamsburg and Mabel between Williamsburg and Barker Creek. A branch from this railroad called the Kalkaska and Southern Railroad was built from Rapid City and extended 33 miles east from Rapid City. You could get on this railroad at Williamsburg or any of the other towns and go north to Petoskey and catch the Grand Rapids and Indiana and go on up to Mackinaw and across the straits by ferry to the railroads in the Upper Peninsula, or you could go south to Traverse City and connect with other railroads and go anywhere in the United States.

Or you could catch the branch from Rapid City called the Kalkaska and Southern and go East from Rapid City through the little towns of Ricker, Rugg, Leiphart, Manan, Kalkaska, Eastman, Spencer, Lands, Sharon, Naples, Butcher and Stratford. Some of these could hardly be called towns, but were stops on the railroad to pick up passengers or freight. Some had Post Offices. This road was built mainly for hauling

Boats and Railroads

logs out of the area. When the timber was all cut, these towns and railroads disappeared.

The Chicago and West Michigan Railroad was taken over by the Pere Marquette around 1900. The Pere Marquette Railroad was taken over by the Chesapeake & Ohio Railroad in 1947 or 1951.

The last passenger train out of Traverse City on this railroad was October 29, 1966. The last freight train on this railroad through Traverse City was on February 20, 1982.

You could board the Chicago and West Michigan Railroad at Williamsburg or any of the little towns along the way, go to Traverse City, change to the Manistee and North Eastern Railroad, go northwest through the little towns of Greilickville, Norrisville, Hatches Crossing, and Solon in Leelanau County, then south to Cedar Run, Lake Ann, Interlochen, Karlin, Nessen City, Copemish and on down to Manistee.

Or you could go north from Solon in Leelanau County on a branch from this railroad through Cedar, Bodus, Schomberg, Elton, and up to Provement, now called Lake Leelanau.

Or you could take the Traverse City, Leelanau and Manistique Railroad from Traverse City through the towns of Greilickville, Norrisville, Bingham, Keswick, Suttons Bay to Northport, and by car ferry to Manistique. This car ferry ran only from 1903 to 1906 or 1908. It carried railroad cars across Lake Michigan to Manistique.

Another railroad called the Empire and Southeastern ran for a short distance from Empire through the little towns of East Empire, Maintop, Jacktown, Peterville, Stormer, and Empire Junction, which were regular stops on the Empire and Southeastern. But it would stop most anywhere to let people on or off.

At Empire Junction it connected up with the Manistee and Northeastern which ran from Empire Junction through Honor and connected up with the main line of the Manistee and Northeastern at, I believe, Platte River Junction.

Figure 1.47: Fast Mail Train at Mabel
Courtesy of Watson Collection

You could board the Manistee and Northeastern at Traverse City and take this road to Empire Junction, change trains and go up to Empire.

This railroad was built for the lumbering business but ended up carrying mostly passengers in the later days. Most of these little towns disappeared when the lumbering business was done.

The Manistee and Northeastern also had a branch from Kaleva along the Manistee River through Buckley to Grayling. I believe this railroad went through Fife Lake.

The Toledo & Ann Arbor Railroad came from downstate through Thompsonville to Frankfort where they had several car ferries they operated to carry the railroad cars across Lake Michigan.

Boats and Railroads

Figure 1.48: Michigan Railroads, 1897
Courtesy of Glenn Neumann

Part II

Early History of Skegemog Point

The Meaning of Skegemog

I have heard of several meanings for Skegemog Point.

> Some say it means where the waters meet.

> Some say it means over the waters.

> Some say it means you can walk or you can ski
> Or you can ski or you can walk.

> Some say it is an Indian word meaning mosquito. Ojibwa pronunciation is Suh-ge-ma-orsaw-ge-may.

The Meaning of Skegmog

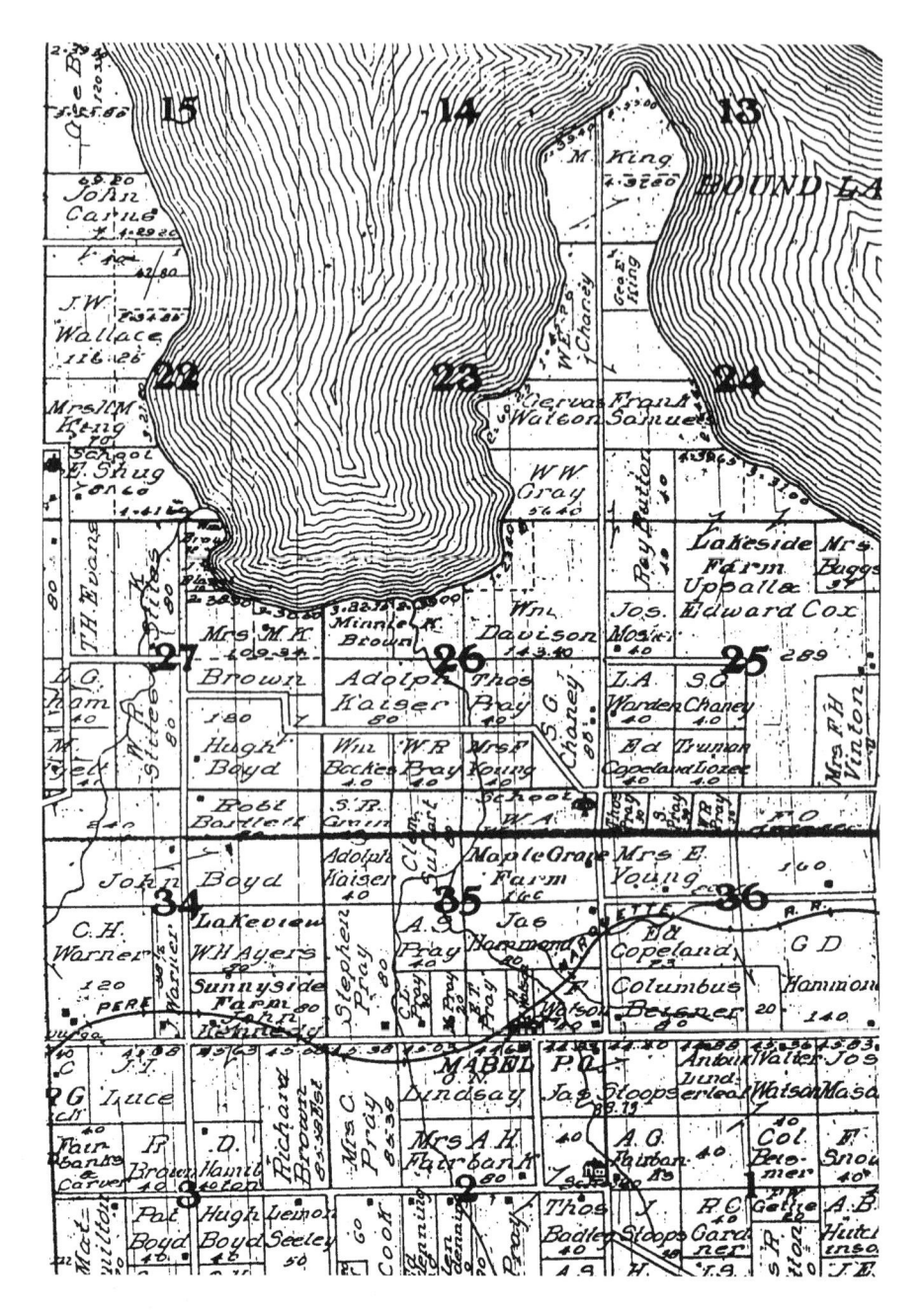

Figure 2.49: 1908 Map of Skegemog Point

Indian History

Skegemog Point may have been inhabited as far back as 8,000 B.C. by a race known as the Palo Indians. Some artifacts have been found on the higher ground to indicate this. The lakes were much higher then and only the highest ground was above water. This was soon after the ice age.

There have been four or five races of people since the ice age. See bibliography: [2, In the Wake of the Ice Age]

The Palo Indians were the first race. They used fluted points. A couple have been found here. The Plano Indians were the second race. They used a point called the Lancelot Point. Several have been found here. They were here from about 7,000 B.C. to about 4,500 B.C.

The Old Copper Indians were here at about the same time as the Boreal Archaic Culture. The Old Copper Indians were the first people to use metal for weapons in this country and perhaps the world. They made weapons out of copper. This copper came from the Upper Peninsula of Michigan.

Then came the Early Woodland Indians, followed by the Late Woodland Indians. They were here from a little before Christ's time 'til the coming of the white man and after. They made triangular points and other shapes.

These races of Indians inhabited the upper Great Lakes region after the ice age and artifacts from all of these races have been found on the Point; early Indians on the higher ground, later Indians on the shores of the lake which was under water at the earlier period.

The Indians held their camp meeting on the Point on the Round Lake side. A trail called the Saginaw Trail came all the way from Saginaw and ended at Elk Lake on the Point. I assume they waded the narrows between Elk and Round Lake and continued on up to Mackinaw.

Indian History

When father was a boy, he was down on the Point on the Round Lake side one day. The Indians had felled a large white pine. One section of it they were making into a log canoe. They had the outside shaped but had not dug the inside out yet. The next time he was down there, it was gone.

Skegemog Point

Elk and Round Lake were named by Abram L. Wadsworth who came to Elk Rapids in the late 1840's. He was a land agent for the Government, also engaged in the resurvey of lands.

Elk Lake, Elk River and Elk Rapids were so named because of a pair of elk horns found by him in the sand at the mouth of the river. He named Round Lake because of its shape and Clam Lake from the vast number of clams found in Clam River. Torch Lake was named by the Indians because of the fishing lights they saw used on the lake. Waswagonink, the Indian name, means a lake of torches.

The water in Elk and Round Lakes was raised by a dam built across the Elk River sometime in the late 1850's or early 1860's. This dam raised the water in the lakes about 28 inches, according to some records. The rapids at Elk Rapids held the water up higher than the Bay. When this dam was built, a hearing was held and the people around the lake went down to approve of it.

When the Samels and Watsons came here in 1855 from Bruce Mines, Ontario, Captain William Samels (he was a captain in the mines) was the father of Mary Samels.

William Samels, Sr. had a sailboat which they towed behind the vessel to Elk Rapids and put it over the rapids into Elk Lake and sailed it up into Round Lake to the west shore where they landed.

William Samels, Sr., a short man, would wade the narrows between Elk and Round Lake before the dam was built at Elk Rapids. He would hold his clothes up over his head.

Round Lake, however, was almost as large as it is now as the dam at Elk Rapids raised it about 28 inches.

Much of the land near the Point in Sections 23 and 24 was a grant from President Filmore in 1853 to a man named Bircherd. After Mr. Bircherd, a man by the name of James Rankin owned the land. Then the Elk Rapids Company, composed of Wirt Dexter and Henry and Ed Noble, bought the land. They took the timber off it. This was in the late 1850's or early 1860's. This was when the dam was built at Elk Rapids.

The Point and all the land back in the country was covered with white and Norway pine. A lot of these white pine were more than 3 1/2 feet through.

Dexter and Nobel had a lumber camp where the quarter line of Section 24 hits Round Lake on property now owned (1981) by Ralph and Doris Waggoner. This lumber camp on Round Lake used teams of oxen to haul the logs to the shore of the lake. I can remember the beech tree where they used to sling the oxen up to put shoes on their feet so they could pull on the ice. The tree still stood there when I was a kid; it is gone now.

The company also had a lumber camp on the Baggs Road on the Cox property and another one across the lake on the Schuler property.

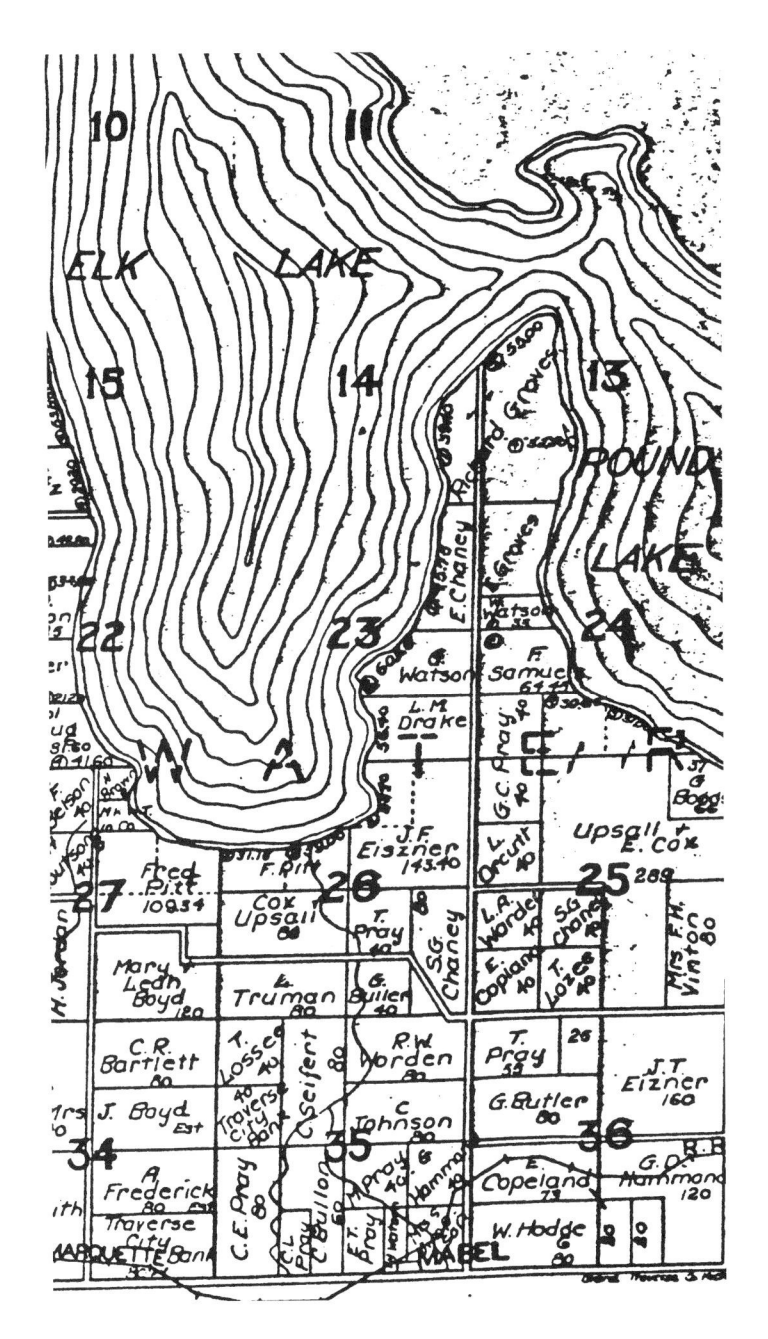

Figure 2.50: Map of Skegemog Point, c. 1926

Skegemog Point

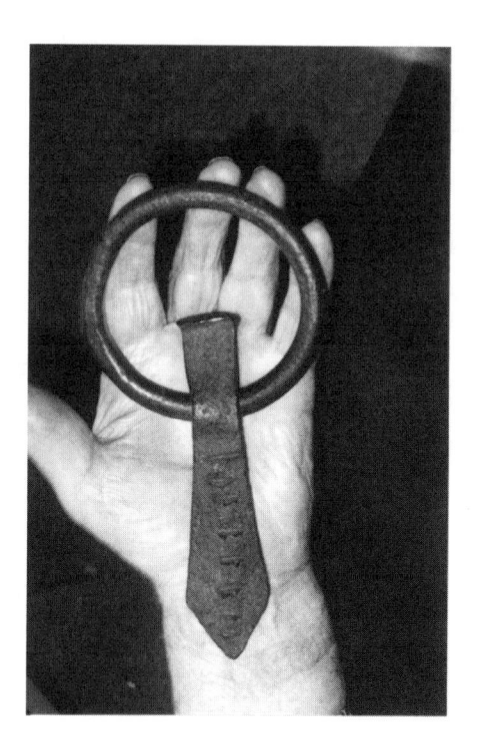

Figure 2.51: Ring and Spike
Courtesy of Samels Collection

Lumbering

The logs for lumber were floated down the lake to their sawmill at Elk Rapids. They would use long poles called boom poles chained end for end. They would string these around a bunch of logs and tie the ends together and tow them down the lake with a steam tug. They would also string the booms around the mouth of Torch River and float the logs down Torch River from Torch Lake into these booms 'til full, then tie the ends together and tow them down the lake. These booms were fastened to two posts, one on each side of the river to catch the logs. I believe these posts can still be seen. These boom poles were hauled back up on the ice in the winter on sleds pulled by teams and stored on the point to be ready for use again the next summer.

After about 1872 when they put the furnace in to make pig iron at Elk Rapids, the people around the lakes and back in the country cut cord wood which was cut four feet long and hauled it to the shore of the lakes and sold it to the company for the furnace. The company hauled the wood down the lakes on their wood scows towed by steam tugs.

To tie the log boom poles together at the ends they had a metal spike with a ring in it. They would drive these spikes in the ends of the boom poles and run a chain through the ring in one pole and through the ring in the next pole.

Lumbering

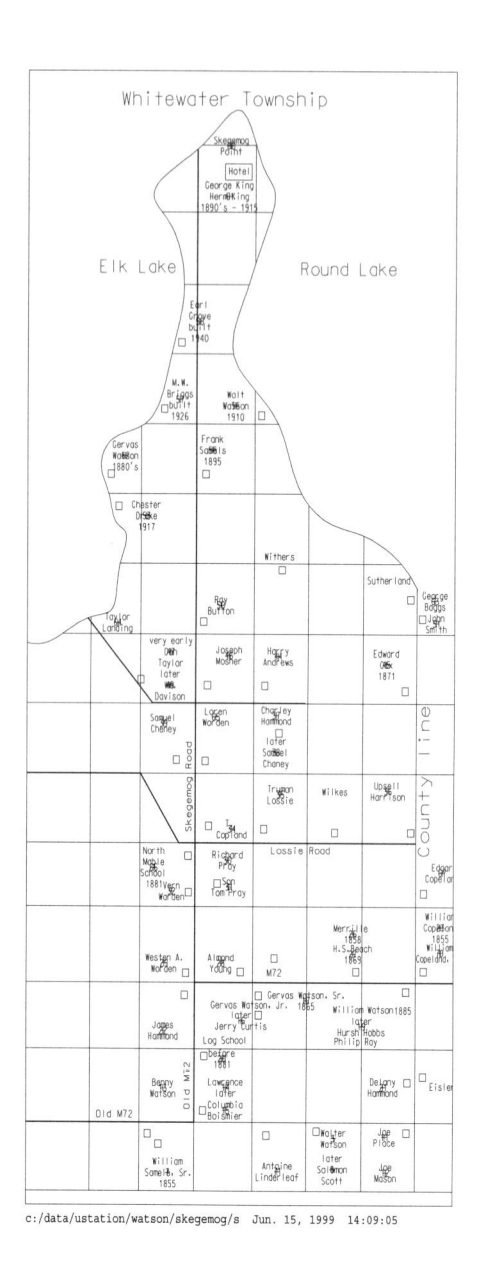

Figure 2.52: Map of Skegemog Point Settlers

People of Skegemog Point

The First Settler

The first man to live near the point that I have heard of, I am not sure of his name but it was either Foster or Sawyer.

My father remembered him having a long low house on Round Lake with a patch of potatoes in front of the house. I do not know if this man owned the land or not, or whether he just lived here and cut wood. Father and his brother hauled two loads of sawdust for this man to pack ice in at one dollar a load. This was the first money father ever earned. This was sometime in the 1880's.

Also around this time the Elk Rapids people held a Fourth of July celebration on the Point. The Elk Rapids Iron Company brought some of their wood scows that they used to haul cord wood down to their furnace on up and anchored them end to end on the Round Lake side to form a dock. The passenger boats made runs to bring up the people from Elk Rapids, and the people back in the country came down to help celebrate. They had races and contests, some in the water, such as they have in an event like this. Fielding Benny Watson came down with a yoke of oxen and fetched a load of relatives with him. He housed the oxen in the log house that Gervas Watson had partly built and walked the rest of the way to the celebration.

Figure 2.53: Pioneers Frank and Mary Samels
Courtesy of Samels Collection

Watson and Samels: Pioneer Families of Whitewater

In September of 1855 the Watson and Samels families came down from Bruce Mines, Ontario, Canada. This included my great-grandfather Gervas Watson, Sr. and his three sons, Fielding (Benny) Watson, William Watson, and Gervas Watson, Jr., and his daughter Miriam Watson Samels, and his granddaughter Mary Samels, one year old. Mary Samels was born at Bruce Mines in 1854; the rest were born in England. His son-in-law Captain William Samels, Sr., who was a Captain in the mines in Canada and England, stayed and worked in the mines a couple of months longer up in Canada and came down on the last boat in the fall.

In England Captain William Samels, Sr. worked in the mines under the sea off Lands End, Cornwall. Gervas Watson, Sr. ran engines, etc. They came over from England in about 1850, the Watsons from Lincolnshire and the Samels from Cornwall, to Bruce Mines and stayed there about five years before coming to Grand Traverse County.

They also brought a woman of French and Indian descent with them from Canada who could talk with the Indians and translate it into English for our folks.

Grandfather Samels had a sailboat which they towed behind the vessel to Elk Rapids and put it over the rapids into Elk Lake and sailed it up into Round Lake and landed on the west side of Round Lake. This was before the dam was built at Elk Rapids to raise the water in the lakes. It was quite a big lake then.

They built a log house on the 160 acres that great-grandfather Watson had bought from the Government for $1.25 an acre on the south side of what is now M-72 between the Baggs and Skegemog Point Roads. The log house was built just west of the county line and south of M-72 where the Ray Boyd house now stands (1986).

They hired a Langworthy with a yoke of oxen from what is now Williamsburg to haul a No. 8 cook stove they had brought with them

People of Skegemog Point

up to the log house. The rest of the stuff they carried up, including eight barrels of flour and some pork. This was a distance of about two miles. They camped for two weeks on the shore of Round Lake while they built the log house. They split out basswood for the floor in this log house.

Captain William Samels, Sr. bought 92 acres of land off the south end of the Skegemog Road in Section 1 and 2 in Town 27 Range 9 West and built a log house where the rest of his family was born including my father, Frank Samels. These were my grandparents.

William Samels, Sr. was born March 27, 1826 in Cornwell, England, and died January 17, 1871. Miriam (Watson) Samels was born July 28, 1833 at Owston Ferry, Lincolnshire, England, and died August 16, 1898. Their children were:

Mary Samels, born at Bruce Mines, Ontario, Canada on May 27, 1854, died at Elk Rapids May 24, 1933.

The rest were born in Whitewater Township, Grand Traverse County:

Jane Samels, born June 8, 1862, died June 8, 1862.
Philip Samels, born August 8, 1864, died December 9, 1935.
Henery Samels, born July 5, 1866, died March 16, 1868.
Frank Samels, born March 28, 1868, died February 24, 1955.
William Henery Samels Jr., born March 29, 1871, died
November 11, 1951.

Early Settlers

Going up the Skegemog Road from the Point, the early settlers were Gervas Watson, Jr. and wife Anne on the shore of Elk Lake. He bought this land in 1883 and moved there shortly after and lived in a log house, and later a frame house.

My father and mother, Frank and Mary Samels, settled here in the fall of 1895 on the land he had bought in 1889.

Ray and Cora Button settled here a little later in the early 1900's.

Daniel and Caroline Taylor were some of the very earliest settlers. He did some preaching. He preached at some of the funerals. He also conducted Sunday School at the North Mabel School house on Sundays. He also did some veterinary work.

Joseph and Phebe Mosher also lived in a log house. They were among the early settlers. Phebe Mosher was Taylor's daughter. Their daughter was Carrie Mosher. Carrie married Perry Scofield.

Loren and Hattie Worden. Hattie Worden was Mosher's daughter.

Ralph and Agnes Worden, Vern Worden, Samuel and Sylvia Chaney.

Another of the early settler families were Richard and Melinda Pray, parents of Thomas Pray.

Thomas and Rose Pray

Westen A. and Sarah Jennie Worden, parents of Loren and Ralph Worden. He had a blacksmith shop on the farm and did some blacksmithing and some carpenter work.

James and Mildred Hammond, early settlers, lived on the west side of the road. The present M-72 goes through about where their door yard was.

People of Skegemog Point

Across the present M-72 on the south end of the Skegemog Road on the west side were Fielding (Benny) and Sarah Watson.

On the east side of the road was a man named Lawrence, followed by Mr. and Mrs. Columbia Boismier on the same place.

On the extreme south end off the Skegemog Road were Captain William, Sr., and Miriam Samels. They were the parents of Frank and William Jr. Samels.

Almost all of these settlers owned the land and raised families here. Almost all of these people lived here in the 1800's sometime after 1855, some extending into the early 1900's. A few were living here the first half of the 1900's, 4 or 5 awhile after 1950.

Others who lived here during the first half of the 20th century for awhile were

    Walter and Margaret Watson
    Claude and Maude Watson, son of Gervas Watson
    Ben and Mabelle Watson, son of Gervas Watson
    Chester and Laura Drake, parents of Chester Drake, Jr.
    Chester Jr. and Mildred Drake
    William and Emma Davison
    Clarence Wilhelm and his father and mother
    Lyle and Osa Orcutt
    Theodore and Alice Chaney
    Edward and Ilah Cox
    Mr. and Mrs. Charley Hammond
    Grover and Cora Hammond
    Herb and Edna Boismier
    Marion and Susan Briggs
    Earl and Emma Grove
    Joe and Ann Duffek
    Ralph and Jean Duffek
    Bert and Lorial Giffen
    Ray and Velma Ashmore
    John F. Eiszner

Hilan and Rea Pray
Don and Floy Norton
Mr. and Mrs. Carson
Mr. and Mrs. Harry Andrews
Mr. and Mrs. Johnson their son Fritz Johnson and wife

Almost all these people owned the property they lived on.

Other people who lived on the Skegemog Road for awhile after 1900 before 1950 but did not own the property:

Mr. and Mrs. Thomas Andrews
Henry Matteson and his mother Stella Matteson
Mr. and Mrs. Warren Thomas
Frank and Geneva Irish
John and Rose Warner

Charles Glendenning had a cabin on the shore of Elk Lake on the Will Chaney property in which he stayed in some winters and fished and sometimes in the summer.

Charles Densteadt also stayed in this cabin some winters.

These are in addition to the caretakers on the Point named on another page.

People of Skegemog Point

People Born and Raised on the Skegemog Road in the first 25 years of the 20th Century

Two or three may not have been born here, but were raised here.

    Amos Lynn Samels, born in 1896
    Frank Dennis Samels, born in 1900
    Ben Wilbur Samels, born in 1907
    Robert Lucius Samels, born in 1912
        sons of Frank and Mary Samels

    Claude Meacham Watson
    Barbara Ann Watson
        children of Ben and Mabelle Watson

    Emma Button
    Clarence Button
        children of Ray and Cora Button

    Lottie Davison
    Ervin Davison
    Melvin Davison
        children of William and Emma Davison

    Garnet Chaney
    Spencer Chaney
    Marjorie Chaney
    Colon Chaney
    Theodore Chaney
    Nellie Chaney
    Alice Chaney
    Laurabelle Chaney
        children of Samual and Sylvia Chaney

    Olive Worden
        raised by Ralph and Agnes Worden

Ila Pray
    daughter of Thomas and Rose Pray

Metta Hammond
Mirla Hammond
    daughters of Grover and Cora Hammond

Irene Boismier
Lawrence Boismier
Nickles Boismier
Ida Boismier
Elenore Boismier
    children of Erb and Edna Boismier

People of Skegemog Point

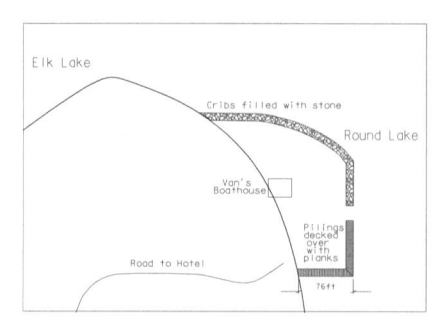

Figure 2.54: Hotel Dock and Boathouse

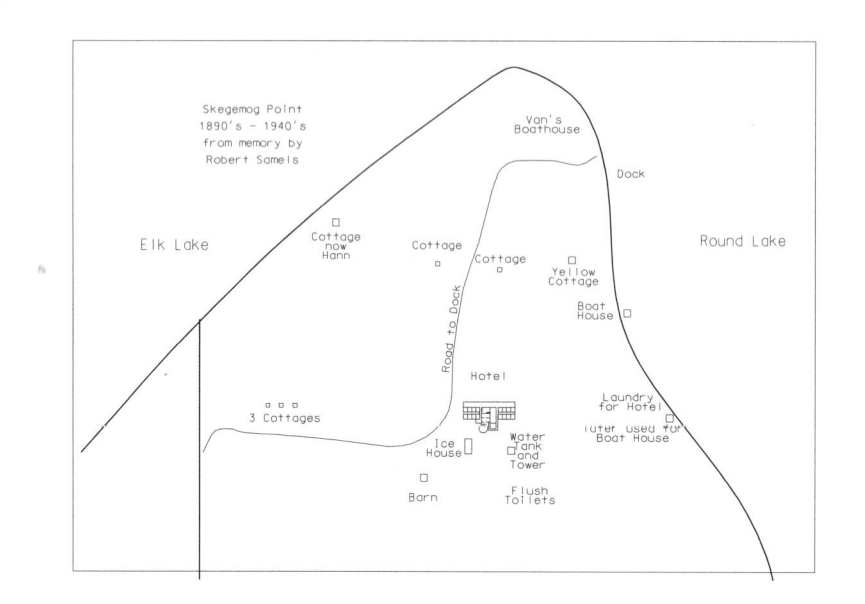

Figure 2.55: Map of the Tip of Skegemog Point

Kings Hotel on the Point

The King family consisted of the old folks, Mr. and Mrs. George King, their son Herm King and his wife Grace. Herm and Grace had one son whose name was Ed King. Herm's wife Grace died while they were on the Point. Later he remarried.

George was a veteran of the Civil War. I believe he was in the Cavalry as mother said he rode horseback some. When he did he would sit up perfectly straight like they did in the Army. They were here on the point before I could remember. Herm came back a couple of times so I met him.

The Kings came in and bought the Point some time after this man lived on the Round Lake side. Just when I do not know, but they built what was called the east lodge in 1897. This was a two story building of 16 rooms, 8 upstairs and 8 downstairs. There was a hall through the center with four rooms on each side. To the west was the house where the Kings lived, which I assume he built first. It had a large living room with a fireplace, also a large room they used for a dining room for the guests, and a small kitchen. There was a building on the southwest corner of this house they used for a summer kitchen they used to prepare food for the guests in.

There were bedrooms upstairs in the main house, some for the help to sleep in. East of the hotel down on the shore of Round Lake was a building they used for a laundry to do the laundry for the hotel in. There was also a small barn on the property.

Rates at the hotel were $1.00 a day with meals. They had some cottages they rented for $20.00 a month with boat. There were either 8 or 9 cottages on the Point, I am not sure which. One cottage burnt up there. Some of these cottages were built by other people. King leased them the lot on a 99 year lease for $10.00 a year.

The Kings had as many as one hundred guests there at times. They built platforms and pitched tents on them to house some people. Guests would come to Elk Rapids and Alden by train, then come the rest of the way by boat. Sometimes when they left, they would hire father to take them to Williamsburg with the horses to catch the train.

Figure 2.56: King's Hotel
Courtesy of Kathi Waggoner Gober

Figure 2.57: King's Hotel Staff
Courtesy of Elk Rapids Area Historical Society

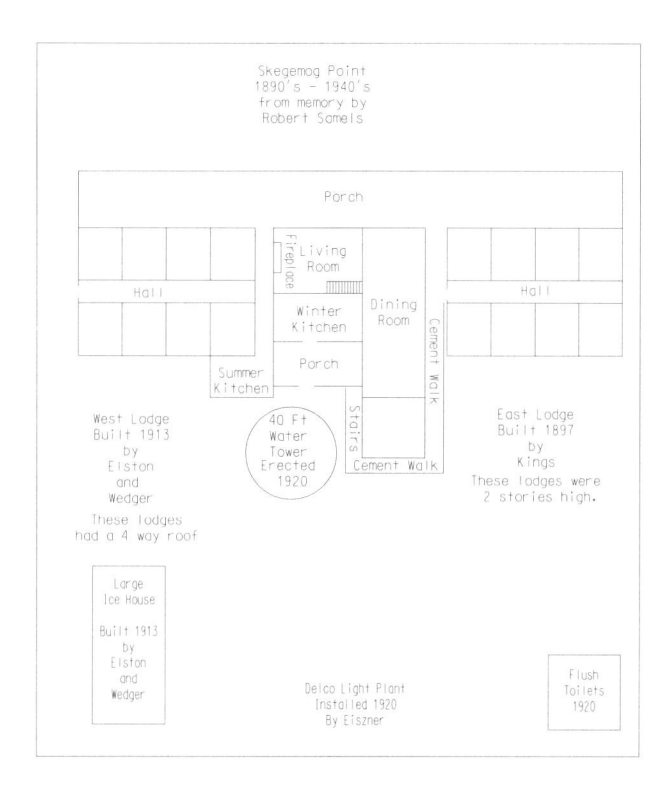

Figure 2.58: Diagram of King's Hotel

Kings ran the hotel 'til about 1913 when they sold the property to a couple of men named Wedger and Elston. One was a Baptist minister, the other a lawyer. They built another lodge of 16 rooms to the west of the other buildings. There was a long porch ran the entire length of both lodges and the house on the north side. They also built a large ice house. They ran the hotel for two summers but could not pay for it and Kings took it back and sold it in 1915 to some Chicago brokers who sold it to John F. Eiszner.

In 1915 a breakwater and dock were added north of the hotel on the East side of the Point. The breakwater, a crib of rocks up to twelve feet wide, was built to about 75 feet out on the north side. The L-shaped dock was built to the south. The pilings were put in place by Joe Hawley from his boat with a pile driver. Braces were built between the pilings, and planks laid on top.

Mr. Eiszner ran the hotel for two or three years, then it lay idle for one year in 1919. In 1920, he put up a 40 foot water tower and built a small building and put in flush toilets. He also put in a Delco light plant. This was the first electricity and flush toilets on the Point.

Mrs. Eiszner ran the hotel in 1920. In 1921 it lay idle. In 1922 a Mr. and Mrs. Berry from Chicago ran the hotel and had a few guests but the advent of the automobile made the hotel business unprofitable. In 1924 my father Frank and brother Dennis roofed the hotel and looked after it. Mr. Eiszner used the hotel for his personal use 'til he sold it in 1926.

In 1926 Mr. Eiszner sold the point to four men named Al Rickerd, Earl Grove, Mr. Butters and George Amiotte. They rented the cottages and boats some. In 1928-29 a Mr. and Mrs. Rose ran the hotel, renting some rooms. From 1930 through 1933, a Mr. and Mrs. Orn Burch rented rooms in the hotel and fed the guests, also rented the cottages.

In 1934 they leased the point to Mr. Kellerman, a singing teacher from Detroit, for a camp for Catholic boys. About 1935, they built the log chapel on the end of the Point for the camp. Mr. Kellerman ran the camp for four years, then gave it up. Then a Mr. Wolf took it over and ran it for three years. In 1941 the Catholic Church leased it for one summer for a camp for students.

It then lay idle during the war 'til 1945 when they had an auction sale and sold off the personal property, then tore down the buildings, all but two cottages which are still standing, and divided the land into lots. The two original cottages built on Skegemog Point when the Kings were there are still standing in 1990. One is now owned by a man named Hanel, the other by a party named McConkey.

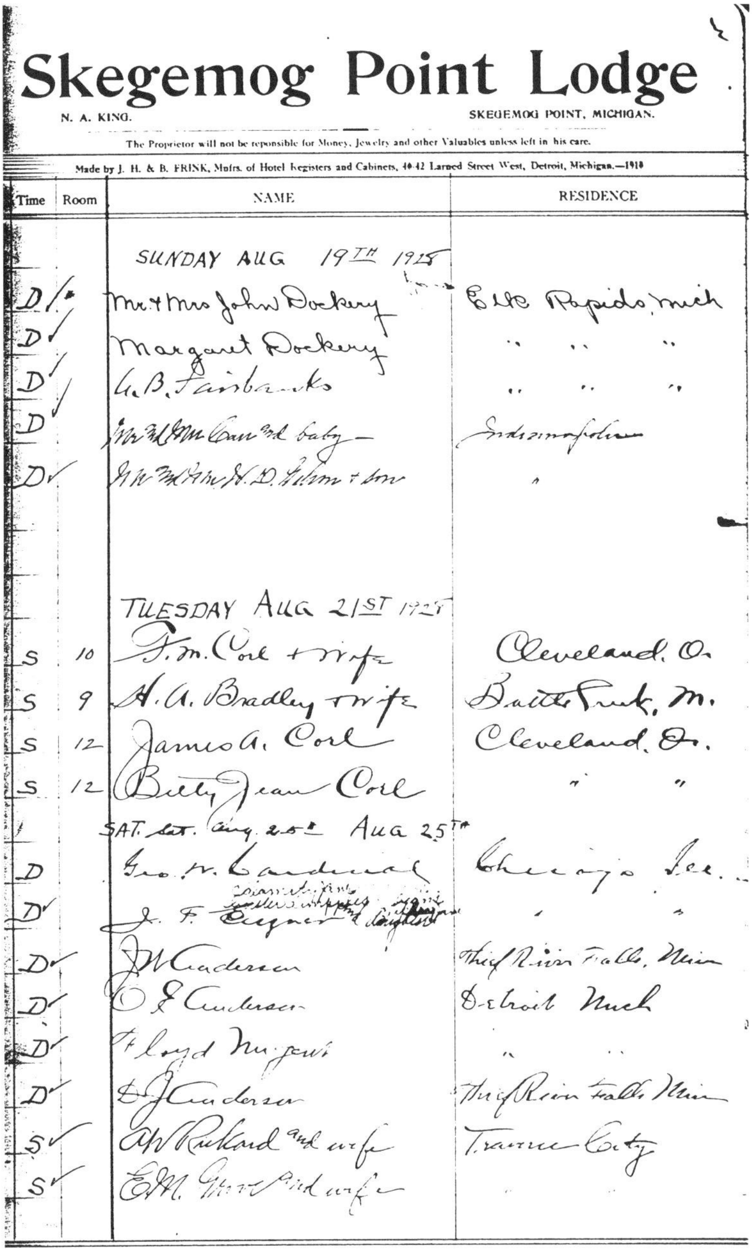

Figure 2.59: Hotel Register, 1928
Courtesy of Doris Waggoner

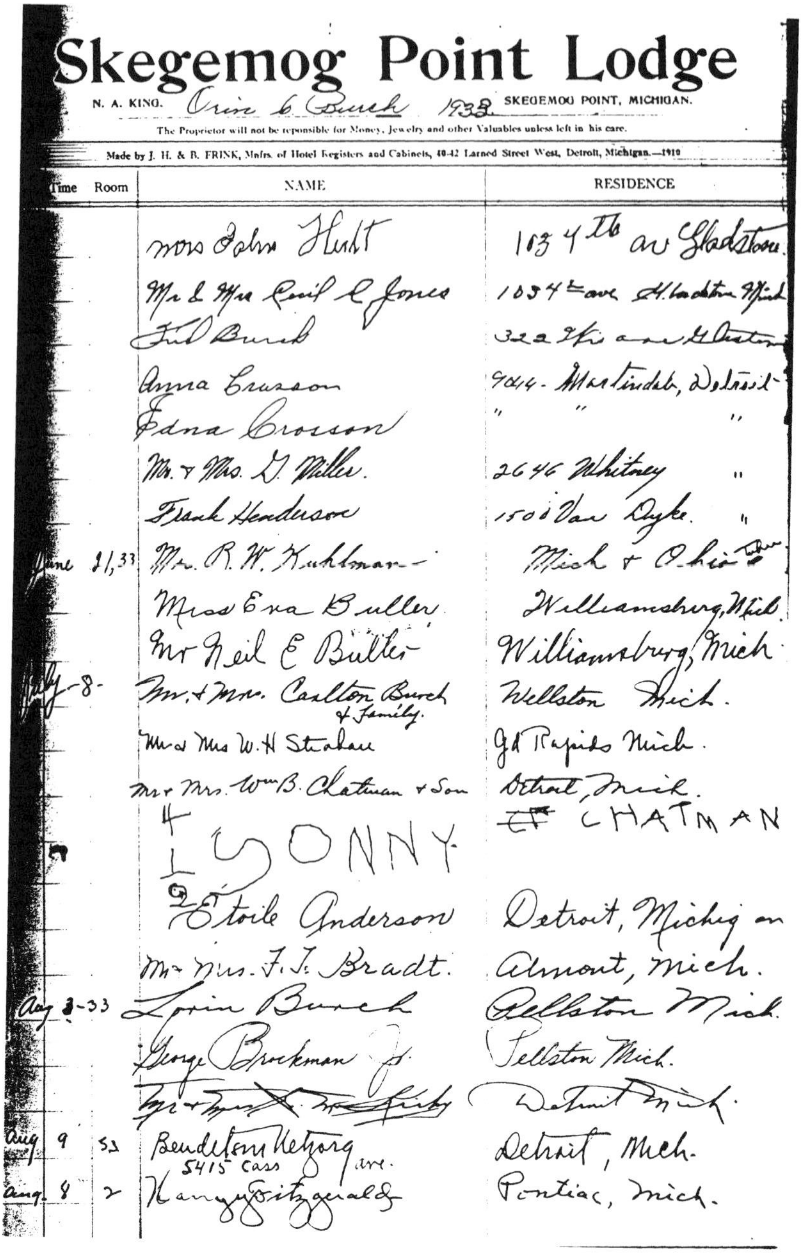

Kings Hotel on the Point

Figure 2.60: Hotel Register, 1933
Courtesy of Doris Waggoner

Caretakers at the Hotel

I do not know what caretakers may have been on the Point when the Kings owned it. The Kings stayed there themselves some winters. After Mr. Eiszner bought it, it was vacant some winters. In the late teens and early twenties, Mr. and Mrs. John Voglies stayed there for a winter or two. Then John and Rose Warner stayed there the year around from 1923 to 1930 except one winter when Charley Densteadt took care of it. This was the winter of 1924. During the summer of 1924 it was idle and my father and brother, Frank and Dennis Samels, looked after it and roofed the main house for Mr. Eiszner.

In 1928-29, a man named Rose and his wife kept some guests in the hotel and rented the cottages.

In 1930 through 1933, Mr. and Mrs. Orn Burch and family took care of it. They kept some guests in the hotel and rented the cottages. Mr. Burch worked for the camp some. They left there in the fall of 1935.

During the winter of 1936 a man named Heberts was caretaker. He left in the spring. Then George and Emma Steele from Detroit were caretakers for about two years, then Loren and Margaret Fuller for a year, then Mr. and Mrs. Dayton Shell for about three years. That was the end of the caretakers. Earl Grove built his house in 1940. He looked after the Point the rest of the time himself 'til it was all sold in lots.

Kings Hotel on the Point

Figure 2.61: Steamer Ruth at Skegemog Point
Courtesy of Kathi Waggoner Gober

Figure 2.62: The Mabel
Courtesy of Elk Rapids Area Historical Society

Boats on the Chain of Lakes: Elk, Round, Torch, Clam, and Bellaire

A history of Skegemog Point would not be complete without a word about the boats that traveled the lakes, hauling both passengers and freight from the mid 1860's to the early teens of the 20th century.

Two of the main boats that ran on the Chain of Lakes were the Odd Fellow run by Joe Hawley, who later changed the name to Ruth after his daughter and the Bellaire run by Ira Sharp. He later named this boat Mabel after his daughter. These two men worked together. This made two boats on the lakes at the same time. These boats traveled this route nearly every day, weather permitting, during the summer. They usually did not run on Sunday unless by charter. You could go to the Point and take a boat to Elk Rapids for a quarter or you could give the Captain a quarter and your grocery list and he would do your shopping for you. King let them use his dock on Round Lake. These boats ran from Elk Rapids to Clam River and some days clear to Bellaire. They hauled both passengers and freight. I believe these two boats ran the longest of any boats on the lakes.

Some mail was carried on these boats from Elk Rapids for the people at the Point. There was a hollow tree near the dock at Skegemog Point. They would place the mail sack in it.

Another boat named Valley Queen also operated in the 1880's from Eastport to Elk Rapids.

In 1885 a boat called the Time started making regular runs between Elk Rapids and Bellaire, hauling both passengers and freight.

John Silkman, a lumberman at the North end of Torch Lake at Brownstown, now called Torch Lake Village, built a steam powered tug which he named the Jennie Silkman after his wife. It plied the lakes at an early date.

A paddle wheel tug called the Albatross operated on the lakes as

Boats on the Chain of Lakes

far back as the mid 1860's.

A boat called the Queen of the Lakes, owned by Dexter and Noble, was built in the 1860's and ran from Eastport to Elk Rapids 'til sometime in the 1880's, making daily trips. It was a sidewheeler built of metal 108 feet long, 34 foot beam and drew 32 inches of water. When the Grand Rapids and Indian Railroad started hauling passengers to Kalkaska in 1873 from the south, a stage ran from Kalkaska to Torch River. Passengers could ride the stage to Torch River and catch the Queen of the Lakes to Elk Rapids or Eastport.

The Queen of the Lakes had staterooms in it. It ran on the lakes from the mid 1860's 'til sometime in the 1880's when it was put over into the Bay. I believe it ran on the Bay some from Elk Rapids to Traverse City, but I heard my father say the Government tied it up as it did not draw water enough to stand the waves on the Bay and Great Lakes. It was then taken down to Holland to run on a lake down there.

Dexter and Noble, who had the sawmill and furnace in Elk Rapids, had three steam tugs on the lakes for towing the logs and wood scows down the lakes to Elk Rapids. One was called the Torch Lake. It had a carved Indian with a drawn bow atop its pilot house. One was called the Elk Lake with a pair of elk horns. One was called the Albatross with a carved albatross in flight.

My Uncle William Samels, Jr. was the Captain of the Albatross for several years. Before him, Fred Laubscher was Captain for awhile. Dexter and Noble had between 20 and 30 of these wood scows that they hauled the wood on down the lakes for the furnace. These scows were about 18 feet wide by 60 feet long with between 4 or 5 foot sides.

Other names of boats I have heard of that ran on the lakes at some time or other were Lizzie Rose, Grass Goose, and Maple Leaf.

Roads of Skegemog Point

The first road to Skegemog Point came down from what is now M-72 on the section line between section 35 and 36. It then went northwesterly down through the Taylor farm to the Taylor landing near the south end of Elk Lake. That is why the farm buildings on the Taylor farm, later the Hubiner property, are back from the present road. From the Taylor landing the road followed the lake shore down to about midway to the Point. It then crossed over to Round Lake, now Skegemog Lake, and followed the Round Lake shoreline to the Point. In some places the Round Lake shore was low and swampy so they had to go farther inland.

In 1895 there was a movement to make this an officially laid out road. But Gervas Watson, who owned all of lot 2, section 23 (in 1985 the west part was owned by L. Kardis and the east 20 acres by Ben and Robert Samels), objected as this road would have gone between his house and the lake. So he got them to put the road the rest of the way down the section line from the quarter line of section 26 between section 25 and 26, sections 23 and 24, and sections 13 and 14. This let all pieces of property on both lakes out to the road.

However, there was need for a road to the south end of Elk Lake. So with the permission of Gervas Watson, who owned all of lot 2, Section 23 now owned the west part by L. Kardis and the east 20 acres by Ben and Robert Samels, a road was laid along the south 8th line of Section 23, Town 28, Range 9 west from the Skegemog Point Road clear to Elk Lake. This was along the south side of lot 2, Section 23, Town 28, Range 9 west.

On November 5 or 6, 1895 Adolph Kaiser, who was highway commissioner of Whitewater Township at the time, brought in a surveyor by the name of Stevens, who lived around Williamsburg down here and who surveyed this line for the road. This road was used by the people who lived around here as a public road for over 60 years to get clear to Elk Lake.

Somewhere around 1914 Gervas Watson decided he would like to take this road up and make it private again. He got up a petition to

Roads of Skegemog Point

take it up. Another petition was got up with signers to leave it public. So the Township Board refused to take up the road and it remained public clear from the Skegemog Point Road to Elk Lake.

I was born off the east end of this road in 1912 and have lived here on the east side of the Skegemog Point Road ever since. Through my father Frank Samels and myself, this is how I know the history of these roads. I have seen two records to verify this.

In 1921 after a winter of no snow and a very dry spring, we had no rain 'til the 7th of July when we got a flood which washed out two culverts on the Skegemog Point Road. One was between M-72 and the Legion Hall; the other was about midway from M-72 to the point. These were culverts made of logs and a plank top. They were replaced with culverts made of cement.

In the spring of 1922 when the snow was thawing up, it caused a pond in the road between our place and the point on the Skegemog Point Road. This pond covered perhaps two or three acres and was too deep to drive through with a car. William Samels was Highway Commissioner of Whitewater Township. He brought a crew of men over and they dug a ditch to Elk Lake to let the water out.

This pond on the Skegemog Point Road was a low place in the area in the spring. When the snow was melting some water would settle here. We would sometimes hear the frogs holler here in the spring of the year.

The Skegemog Point Road for a long time was a two track road with ruts. Sometime in the later 1920's they started to improve it from where M-72 crosses it going north. They graded it some and put some gravel on it. They got perhaps half of the way down to the point in the later 1930's and 1940's.

Up until the early 1930's, the township maintained the roads. Then by a state law they turned the roads all over to the counties to maintain.

In 1949 and 1950, the County Road Commission graded the entire road from M-72 north, and in 1951 they paved it with blacktop.

My father and mother, Frank and Mary Samels, moved on this place where I was born in November of 1895 and both lived here until their death.

These roads were established by the pioneers who first settled here so that they and their descendants would always have access to the lakes. Some of these roads, by legal means or otherwise, however, have been closed to the people who live here.

I do not have a history of the Lossie Road as to when it was laid out. But it was established along with the other roads by the early settlers. One of the early settlers, if not the first to settle on the Lossie Road, was a party by the name of Wilks. Perhaps this is not the correct spelling. They were Thomas Pray's grandparents. This was between the Skegemog Road and the Baggs Road.

The road from the Skegemog Road west to the Cook Road is now called the Lossie Road. We used to call it the Swamp Road. The early settlers used it as a short cut across the swamp.

My father used to take wheat to Elk Rapids to the flour mill to get it ground into flour. He would go across this swamp road to the Cook Road with the horses as it would save about two miles each way to Elk Rapids. This was an all-day trip with a team of horses. People used to go across on this road with the Model T Ford to fish the creeks after cars came in.

Roads of Skegemog Point

Figure 2.63: South Mabel School Students, 1914
South Mabel School Teacher, Bertha Orcutt
Front Row: Ula Parks, Alden Pray, Kenneth Watson, John Watson
Back Row: Ada Watson, Lena Button, Ruth Button, Octavia (Bunny) Pray

Courtesy of Kathi Waggoner Gober

The First Automobile

Figure 2.64: Rose and Ed Glendenning's First Auto
Courtesy of Karon Anderson

The first automobile down the Skegemog Road was a Franklin. It was air cooled. It was owned by William Chaney. It came down as far as our place (Samels) in 1909. I do not know if he went any further or not. This was when Walter Watson bought the land north of our place from William Chaney which he owned for many years. When a car went clear to the Point I do not know. The road was pretty rough, only two ruts at that time. I remember when several of the people around here bought their first car.

The first airplane we saw over Skegemog Point here was in the summer of 1918.

Figure 2.65: North Mabel School
Courtesy of Samels Collection

Figure 2.66: North Mabel School Class, 1922
Courtesy of Samels Collection

Schools of Skegemog Road

The first school on Skegemog Road was a log building located on the east side near the south end of Skegemog Road on property now owned (1987) by Jack Bates. Just when it was built I do not know but it was used before 1881.

In 1881 there was a need for a new and larger building as father said this log school was filled to capacity with boys and girls. Some older boys and girls even went to school here to get some learning. This was where father got most of his education.

So in 1881 it was decided to build a new building. Since this district extended from the Point clear out to the edge of the pine plains, it was quite a way for some of the children to walk. It was decided to divide the district into two districts. The south end built a school house on what is now called the Deal Road. It was later called the South Mabel School as the town of Mabel had not yet been established. The North end built a school building on the southwest corner of the Skegemog and Lossie Roads. It was later called the North Mabel School.

The South Mabel School was run 'til about 1920 when it was consolidated with the Williamsburg School.

The North Mabel School was run 'til 1941 or 1942 when they transported the kids to the Williamsburg School.

These schools had grades from kindergarten through the eighth grade, all in one room.

The 1922 photograph of the North Mabel School Class shows in the back row, the teacher, Stella (Copeland) Dockery, and students; Alice Chaney, Harvey Giffen, Walter Cox, Ruth Dornboss, middle row, Homer Giffen, Edward Giffen, Lynn Orcutt, Olive Worden, Laurabelle Chaney, bottom row, Neil Buller, Nickles Boismier, Lowell Ray, Lawrence Boismier and Robert Samels.

In the North Mabel one-room school on the Skegemog Point Road, we studied the following subjects: Grammar, Civics, Arithmetic, United States History, Agriculture, Orthography (spelling), Government, Physiology, Geography, Spelling, Writing, and Reading. We had some art. When we finished both the seventh and eighth grades, we had to go over to the Williamsburg School and take a state exam in both grades. The tests were sent in to the county school commissioner. He checked them over and sent out a certificate of promotion to them that passed the tests. This was in the early twenties when I went to school there.

Teachers of the North Mabel School

North Mabel School was built in 1881 and later was called Round Lake School.

1906	Cora (Pray) Hammond
1907	Addie Crisp
1908	Mabel (Beckwith) Pray
1909	Helen Whistson
1910	Daisy Lahr
1911	Bertha Orcutt
1912	Eunice L. Primeau
1913-14	Alma Breithaup
1915	Hazel Page
	Ethel Pray
1916-17-18	Catherine Dafoe
1919-20	Margie Chaney
1921-22	Marcella (Clow) Butler
1923-24	Stella (Copeland) Dockery
1925-26	Doris (Copeland) Laming
1927-28	Irene (Skiver) Cox
1929	Margaret Armstrong
1930	Alphri Gardner
1931-32-33	Hazel Metty
1934	Ila (Pray) Cox
	Eva Buller

The school closed and students went to Williamsburg in 1942-43.

Mabel

Figure 2.67: Mabel Church Group
Alva Breightup, Bill Copeland, Cora and Lucille Copeland, Mrs. Hattie Moshier Worden, Dick Copeland, Mrs. Bertha Peterson, and Mrs. Leatherby.
Courtesy of Ina Robb

Mabel was a little town established when the railroad went through in 1892. It was located on the Watson Road west of the south end of the Skegemog Road and a little west of where the Mabel Road intersects the Watson Road. A flowing well, which is still there, was drilled in 1908 and was about the strongest flowing well in the state. It flows into Battle Creek and thus into Elk Lake. This creek is correctly spelt Battle Creek and not Bottle Creek as it is spelt on some maps.

Mabel was in Section 35, town 28, range 9 West. It was named after Mabel Bates, daughter of a Traverse City publisher. Mabel consisted of a sawmill, a shingle mill, a store, and Post Office for awhile.

Bert Johnson had a blacksmith shop at Mabel one hundred years ago. Mones Linderleaf worked for Bert Johnson in his blacksmith shop and got quite handy at blacksmithing.

Carl Hasting had a store at Mabel. It was a two story building with living quarters upstairs.

Figure 2.68: Flowing Well at Mabel, 1908
This well, drilled with two inch pipe for Gilbert Pray by Gardner and Son, spouted eight feet high and was believed to have the strongest flow of any in the state.
Courtesy of Grand Traverse Pioneer and Historical Society

The Beauty Spot - Also known as Amos Wood's Landing

Figure 2.69: Beauty Spot
Courtesy of Elk Rapids Area Historical Society

On the west shore of Round (Skegemog) Lake on Skegemog Point perhaps 80 rods south of the north line of Section 24 was an open space which the early settlers called the Beauty Spot. The early settlers back in the country would go down here to have picnics. There was a large tree here of either maple or beech. It was also called Amos Wood's Landing or Ames Wood Landing.

Amos Wood was one of the earliest settlers of Elk Rapids. He had a little shanty on this landing where he stayed in and I believe cut wood.

Amos Wood lived to be about 101 years old.

There was another Wood by the name of, I believe, Enoch Wood who may have been the one this landing was named after. He lived around Elk Rapids.

Amos Wood lived around Elk Rapids for many years.

The Beauty Spot

Figure 2.70: Skegemog Point Road, 1908
Courtesy of Kathi Waggoner Gober

Bibliography

[1] *The Traverse Region, Historical and Descriptive, with Illustrations of Scenery and Portraits and Biographical Sketches*, H.R. Page & Co., Chicago, 1884.

[2] Gardner, Paul, "In the Wake of the Ice Age," *American Archaeology*, Summer, 1999; 34-35.

[3] Hayes, E.L., C.E., *Atlas of Grand Traverse County Michigan*, C. O. Titus, Philadelphia, 1881.

Index

Amiotte, George, 124
Andrews, Harry, 117
Andrews, Thomas, 117
Armstrong, Margaret, 138
Arnold, Amelia Langworthy, 45
Arnold, J. W., 43, 45
Ashmore, Ray, 116
Ashmore, Velma, 116
Aslett, Mr., 64, 83

Babcock, Dr., 57
Baggs, Florence, 81
Baggs, George, 79, 81
Baggs, John, 79, 81
Baggs, Millie Smith, 80, 81
Bartlett, Frank, 68
Bartok, Mr., 24
Bates, Jack, 137
Bates, Mabel, 77, 139
Bates, Thomas T., 77
Baucus, William, 43
Beach, H. I., 44
Beach, H. L., 42
Beach, H. S., 82
Beadle, Mr., 24
Beckwith, Milton, 14
Beebe, A. C., 88
Beebe, Charley, 25
Beebe, D. P., 88
Beecham, Horace K., 46
Beecham, Lucy Gurnee, 46
Berry, Mr., 124
Bircherd, Mr., 106
Bloodgood, Emily Griffis, 45
Bloodgood, James O., 42, 45, 69
Bockes, William H., 86, 87
Boismier, Abb, 49

Boismier, Alice, 49
Boismier, Art, 49
Boismier, Columbia, 49, 116
Boismier, Edna, 116, 119
Boismier, Elenore, 119
Boismier, Erb, 119
Boismier, Herb, 116
Boismier, Ida, 119
Boismier, Irene, 119
Boismier, Laun, 49
Boismier, Lawrence, 119, 137
Boismier, Nickles, 119, 137
Boismier, Rose, 49
Boismier, Urb, 49
Boismier, William, 49
Boman, Mr., 45
Boyd, Elaine Ray, 81
Boyd, Granny, 43
Boyd, Hugh, 43, 46
Boyd, Jack, 30
Boyd, James, 43, 46
Boyd, John, 43, 46
Boyd, Pat, 30
Boyd, Patrick, 43, 46
Boyd, Ray, 80, 81, 113
Breightup, Alva, 139
Breithaup, Alma, 138
Brennaman, John, 86
Briggs, Marion, 116
Briggs, Susan, 116
Broadfoot, Mr., 24
Broomhead, Aaron, 43, 45
Broomhead, Burl, 36
Broomhead, Charley, 43, 45
Broomhead, George, 43, 46
Brown, Am, 45

INDEX

Brown, Art, 43, 45, 49
Brown, Blyth, 50
Brown, Carl, 50
Brown, Charlotte Watson, 47
Brown, Fred, 50
Brown, George, 42, 44
Brown, Howard, 32, 50, 67
Brown, Lonson, 43, 46
Brown, Mary Langworthy, 44
Brown, Nellie Vinton, 45, 58
Brown, Ora, 47, 50
Brown, Paul, 50
Brown, Richard, 43, 45, 49
Brown, Russel, 45
Buller, Dora Young, 82
Buller, Eva, 82, 138
Buller, Garnet, 51
Buller, Garnet, Jr., 82
Buller, Garnet, Sr., 82
Buller, Gladys, 82
Buller, Neil, 50, 82, 137
Bunce, C. W., Dr., 57
Bunce, Earl, 57
Burch, Ora, 127
Burch, Orn, 124
Butler, Marcella Clow, 138
Butters, Mr., 124
Button, Ambrose, 43, 45, 49
Button, Berth, 49
Button, Charley, 49
Button, Clarence, 118
Button, Cora, 115, 118
Button, Earl, 49
Button, Edith, 49
Button, Em, 49
Button, Emma, 118
Button, Frank, 49
Button, Harry, 49
Button, James, 49
Button, Jerome, 45
Button, Jo Ann, 49
Button, Lena, 134
Button, Mate, 49
Button, Ray, 115, 118
Button, Ruth, 134

Button, Win, 49

Caldwell, Mr., 23
Campeau, A., 14
Carmien, Aubrey, 73
Carns, John, 43, 45
Carns, Lucinda Hawley, 45
Carrier, Mr., 24
Carson, Mr., 117
Champney, Rolly, 86
Chaney, Alice, 116, 118, 137
Chaney, Colon, 118
Chaney, Garnet, 118
Chaney, Laurabelle, 118, 137
Chaney, Margie, 138
Chaney, Marjorie, 118
Chaney, Mr., 87
Chaney, Nellie, 118
Chaney, Samual, 118
Chaney, Samuel, 115
Chaney, Spencer, 118
Chaney, Sylvia, 115, 118
Chaney, Theodore, 116, 118
Chaney, Will, 117
Chaney, William, 135
Clark, Dr., 57
Clark, Mr., 24
Clement, Elisha W., 88
Clement, Mr., 13, 45, 51
Clow, Robert, 68
Cobb, Mr., 33
Conant, Timothy, 43, 46
Cook, Bill, 36
Cooper, John E., 25
Copeland, Bill, 139
Copeland, Cora, 81, 82, 139
Copeland, Edgar, 79
Copeland, Edward, 81, 82
Copeland, Henry, 79
Copeland, Lawrence, 81
Copeland, Lucille, 139
Copeland, Maddie, 81
Copeland, Marjorie, 81
Copeland, Mary, 81
Copeland, Mary Swaney, 79
Copeland, Mr., 21

Copeland, Richard, 81, 139
Copeland, Rose, 79
Copeland, Ruby, 81
Copeland, Thomas, 79
Copeland, William, 50
Copeland, William, Jr., 79, 81
Copeland, William, Sr., 42, 79, 81, 86, 87
Cox, Amelia, 81, 83
Cox, Edward, 46, 79–81, 116
Cox, Fanny, 81
Cox, Henry, 81
Cox, Ila Pray, 138
Cox, Ilah, 116
Cox, Irene, 81
Cox, Irene Skiver, 138
Cox, Joe, 81
Cox, Lewis, 81–83
Cox, Mary, 50, 79
Cox, Millie, 46, 79, 81
Cox, Nora, 81
Cox, Upsell, 16, 79, 81
Cox, Walter, 81, 137
Crisp, Addie, 138
Crisp, William, 43, 46
Cronin, Cornelius, 87
Cross, Joel, 43, 46, 51
Cross, Mr., 58
Cross, Vet, 43, 46, 51
Curtis, Josiah, 43, 44, 82

Dafoe, Catherine, 138
Davison, Emma, 116, 118
Davison, Ervin, 118
Davison, Lottie, 118
Davison, Melvin, 118
Davison, William, 116, 118
Dean, Richard, 72
Dempsey, Mr., 88
Densteadt, Charles, 117, 127
Desmond, Peter, 87
Devries, Albert, 13, 64
Dexter, Hoyt, 33
Dexter, Wirt, 14, 17, 106
Dockery, Alice, 81
Dockery, Patrick, 88

Dockery, Stella (Copeland), 137
Dockery, Stella Copeland, 138
Dockery, Thomas, 32, 81
Donahue, Mr., 88
Dornboss, Ruth, 137
Drake, Chester, 116
Drake, Chester, Jr., 116
Drake, Clinton, 68, 72, 73
Drake, Laura, 116
Drake, Mildred, 116
Duffek, Ann, 116
Duffek, Jean, 116
Duffek, Joe, 116
Duffek, Ralph, 116
Dunbar, Eber J., 9
Durga, William R., 13, 42, 45, 51

Eaton, A. W., 11, 13, 43, 46
Eaton, Charley, 11
Ehle, Dr., 57
Eisler, Jacob, 81
Eisler, Margaret, 81
Eisler, Mr., 80
Eiszner, J. R., 83
Eiszner, John F., 116, 123, 124, 127
Ellies, Mr., 123
Ellis, Dr., 57
Ennest, James, 64
Evarett, James, 79, 85

Fairbanks, A. K., 42–44, 49
Fairbanks, Albert, 77
Fairbanks, Andrew, 42–44, 49
Fairbanks, Dell, 35, 43, 45, 49
Fairbanks, Doan Broomhead, 45, 49
Fairbanks, Emeline Eastman, 44, 49
Fairbanks, Mary Thompson, 44, 49
Fairbanks, Ora, 49
Fairbanks, Sarah Broomhead, 44, 49
Fairbanks, William, 43, 45, 49
Farrell, Harry, 32
Fife, William H., 7
Filmore, President James, 106
Follett, J. I., 14, 43
Follett, J. I., Sr., 44
Follett, James L., 43

INDEX

Follett, James S., 14
Follett, James S., Jr., 44
Foster, Mr., 111
Fuller, Loren, 127
Fuller, Margaret, 127
Fundy, Isaac, 41, 44

Gaines, Sumner, 68
Gardiner, Arch, 28
Gardner, Mr., 77
Gardner, R. C. M., 68
Garner, Alphri, 138
Gauntlett, Dr., 57
Gay, Doris Brown, 67
Gay, Earl, 68, 72, 73
Gay, Michael, 14, 33
Gibson, William, 88
Giffen, Bert, 116
Giffen, Edward, 137
Giffen, Harvey, 137
Giffen, Homer, 137
Giffen, Lorial, 116
Gillett, Eli, 88
Glendenning, Charles, 117
Glendenning, Ed, 47, 135
Glendenning, Edward, 48
Glendenning, Hattie, 51
Glendenning, Helen Shaw, 45
Glendenning, Mabel, 48
Glendenning, Matthew, 45
Glendenning, Rose, 48
Glendenning, Rose , 135
Glendenning, Rose Watson, 47
Goodrich, Mr., 83
Grove, Earl, 116, 124, 127
Grove, Emma, 116

Hamilton, John, 43, 46
Hamilton, Margaret Bell, 46
Hammond, Albert, 50
Hammond, Cassie, 80
Hammond, Charley, 50, 116
Hammond, Cora, 116, 119
Hammond, Cora Pray, 138
Hammond, Delany, 80, 81
Hammond, Ed, 50

Hammond, Godfrey D., 50
Hammond, Grover, 50, 116, 119
Hammond, James, 43, 44, 50, 115
Hammond, Mary Cox, 80, 81
Hammond, Metta, 119
Hammond, Mildred, 44, 50, 115
Hammond, Mirla, 119
Hanel, Mr., 124
Hannah, Perry, 33, 34
Hannah, W., 73
Hanson, Mr., 83
Harrison, Emma, 79
Harrison, Mary, 79
Harrison, Rebecca Copeland, 46
Harrison, Upsell, 43, 46, 79–81
Hasting, Carl, 51, 77, 140
Haviland, J.B., 7
Hawley, Frank, 46
Hawley, Joe, 124, 129
Haynes, L. A., 88
Heberts, Mr., 127
Hewitt, William, 86, 87
Hoard, Mahlon, 43, 46, 63
Hobbs, Charley, 67
Hobbs, Hursh, 80, 81
Hobbs, Mary, 81
Hobbs, Mary Harrison, 80
Hobbs, Opel, 80
Hobbs, Upsel, 67, 80
Hogeland, Ed, 46, 51
Holdsworth, William, Dr., 56
Holsworth, Frank, Dr., 57
Hough, William, 88
Houghton, Mr., 82
Hoxsie, A., 9
Hoxsie, Dennis, 79
Hoyt, Anne, 49
Hoyt, Byron, 49, 77, 86
Hoyt, Hattie, 49
Hoyt, Lute, 49, 67
Hoyt, Ross, 49
Humphrey, George, 43, 45, 49
Hunley, Thomas, 88

Irish, Frank, 117
Irish, Geneva, 117

Johnson, Alfred, 67
Johnson, Bert, 139
Johnson, Fritz, 117
Johnson, Mr., 82, 117
Johnson, Thomas, 88

Kaiser, Adolf, 25, 49
Kaiser, Adolph, 131
Kaiser, Miriam Watson, 49
Kardis, L., 131
Kellerman, Mr., 124
Kellogg, A. T., 88
King, Ed, 121
King, George, 121
King, Grace, 121
King, Herm, 121
King, Mr., 129
Kramer, Martin, 25
Krogel, Mrs., 68

Lackey, Ina, 36
Lackey, Mrs., 36
Lahr, Daisy, 138
Laming, Doris Copeland, 138
Lamson, Sarah, 47
Lancaster, Thomas, 88
Landon, John, 45
Langworthy, Amelia, 43
Langworthy, Amon, 11, 41, 44
Langworthy, H. A., 11
Langworthy, H. L., 41
Langworthy, Martha Welton, 44
Langworthy, Mary, 42
Langworthy, Mr., 114
Langworthy, William, 41, 44
Laubscher, Fred, 18
Laubscher, Mary, 47
Lawrence, Mr., 43, 45, 49, 116
Lawrence, Polly, 45, 49
Lay, Mr., 33
Leatherby, Jack, 43
Leatherby, Mrs., 139
Leavitt, Mr., 42
Letherby, John H., 87
Linderleaf, Antoine, 47
Linderleaf, Edward, 47

Linderleaf, Engle, 47, 49
Linderleaf, Mary Samels, 47
Linderleaf, Miriam, 47
Linderleaf, Mones, 47, 139
Lindsey, Orin, 20
Lossee, Julia, 83
Lossee, Truman, 83
Louden, Mr., 23

Marsh, Oscar, 63
Mason, Joe, 80, 81
Mason, John, 87
Mason, Lavina Pray, 80, 81
Mason, Lurance, 81
Mason, William, 81
Matteeson, Henry, 117
Matteson, Stella, 117
McConkey, Mr., 124
McCune, Ed, 46, 51
McNulty, Mr., 89
Merrill, J. M., 42, 44, 82
Merrill, William, 43, 46
Metty, Hazel, 138
Mitchell, Mr., 33
Moran, Martin, 86
Moran, Mr., 87
Morgan, Birney J., 24
Mosher, Carrie, 115
Mosher, Joseph, 45, 115
Mosher, Phebe Taylor, 45, 115
Murray, G. F., 24

Noble, Ed, 14, 17, 106
Noble, Henry, 14, 17, 33, 106
Noble, Oscar, 14
Norton, Don, 117
Norton, Floy, 117
Noteware, Hiram, 46

Odell, Philander, 42–44
Omen, Phil, 68
Orcutt, Bertha, 134, 138
Orcutt, Burdette, 82
Orcutt, Lyle, 82, 116
Orcutt, Lynn, 137
Orcutt, Olive, 82

INDEX

Orcutt, Osa, 82, 116

Page, Hazel, 138
Palmer, Lewis, 14
Parks, Ula, 134
Payne, Mr., 33
Perkins, S. W., 65
Peterson, Bertha, 139
Petertyl, A. J., 23
Petertyl, Victor, 23
Pitcher, Zina, Dr., 57
Place, Joseph, 43, 45, 80, 81
Plat, Mr., 13
Post, Philip, 9, 86
Pray, Alden, 134
Pray, Andrew, 46, 50, 77
Pray, Ashley, 50
Pray, Austin, 18, 48
Pray, Big Ed, 36, 46, 50
Pray, Carrie, 50
Pray, Carrie Estes, 46, 50
Pray, Charles, 48
Pray, Cliff, 50
Pray, Clint, 50
Pray, Cora, 50
Pray, Effey, 50
Pray, Emma Stites, 50
Pray, Ethel, 50, 138
Pray, George, 50
Pray, Gilbert, 50, 67, 77, 140
Pray, Gladys, 50
Pray, Hazen, 50
Pray, Helen, 50
Pray, Hilan, 117
Pray, Hobart, 48
Pray, Ila, 119
Pray, Larry, 50
Pray, Linney, 13
Pray, Little Ed, 18, 47, 50
Pray, Mabel Beckwith, 138
Pray, Mary Broomhead, 46, 50
Pray, Melinda, 45, 50, 115
Pray, Mort, 50
Pray, Oliver, 50, 83
Pray, Orly, 50
Pray, Rea, 117

Pray, Rebecca, 48
Pray, Rebecca Watson, 47, 50
Pray, Richard, 43, 45, 50, 115
Pray, Rose, 115, 119
Pray, Rose Young, 82
Pray, Steve, 43, 45, 50
Pray, Thomas, 50, 82, 83, 115, 119, 133
Pray, Warren, 50, 82
Pray, William, 43, 47, 50
Primeau, Eunice L., 138
Pulcipher, John, 7

Randel, Mr., 82
Randolph, Leroy, 65
Rankin, James, 106
Ray, Cassie Hammond, 81
Ray, Ladore Whiteford, 81
Ray, Lowell, 81, 137
Ray, Philip, 32, 80–82
Rex, Rob, 25
Rice, Lue, 24
Rickerd, Al, 124
Rickerd, John, 43, 46
Rickerd, Lafe, 43, 46
Rickerd, Len, 13, 43, 46, 51
Robinson, Mr., 82
Rose, Emery, 27
Rose, Mr., 124, 127
Ross, Norman, 88

Samels, Amos Lynn, 118
Samels, Ben Wilbur, 25, 118, 131
Samels, Eldon, 65
Samels, Frank, 27, 31, 47, 71, 113–116, 118, 124, 127, 132
Samels, Frank Dennis, 25, 38, 118, 124, 127
Samels, Henery, 47, 114
Samels, Jane, 114
Samels, Mary, 41, 47, 105, 113, 114, 133
Samels, Mary Laubscher, 113, 115, 118
Samels, Miriam Watson, 3, 41, 44, 47, 113, 114, 116
Samels, Philip, 47, 114

INDEX

Samels, Robert Lucius, 118, 131, 137
Samels, William, 47, 71
Samels, William Henery, Jr., 114
Samels, William, Capt., 19, 37, 41, 43, 44, 105, 113, 114, 116
Samels, William, Jr., 18, 32, 47, 116, 130, 132
Sawyer, Mr., 82, 111
Schlagel, Julian, 80
Schlagel, Loree, 80
Scofield, Bernie, 19
Scofield, C. T., 14, 63
Scofield, Charles, 42
Scofield, Charles Truemain, 46
Scofield, Cordelia, 46
Scofield, Daniel, 42
Scofield, Daniel B., 43, 46
Scofield, Daniel B., Rev., 42
Scofield, Laura, 11, 42, 46
Scofield, Perry, 115
Scofield, Truman, 20
Scott, Solomon, 47
Seeley, Bertha, 47
Seeley, Chance, 66
Seeley, Daymon, 67, 73
Seeley, Evert, 67, 73
Seeley, Lucy, 73
Seeley, Martha Depew, 46
Seeley, Samuel, 43, 46
Selkirk, George, 43, 46
Selkirk, Jeanette Robertson, 46
Shane, Tom, 24
Sharp, Ira, 129
Shaw, Charley, 68
Shell, Dayton, 127
Silkman, John, 129
Silver, Bert, 53
Silver, Dick, 53, 63
Silver, G. Lote, 53
Silver, Glen, 53
Silver, Harry, 53
Silver, Jim, 53
Simmons, Link, 89
Smith, John, 79, 81
Smith, Millie Eisler, 79, 81

Sours, Joseph, 41, 44
Sours, Lowell, 41
Sours, Mary Lowell, 44
Spencer, Sarah, 42, 69
Springstein, W. L., Dr., 43, 46, 57
Stafford, Mr., 83
Steele, Emma, 127
Steele, George, 127
Steve, J., 87
Stevens, Mr., 131
Stites, Empire, 37, 43, 45
Stites, Kossuth, 12, 13, 43, 45
Stites, Newton, 43, 45
Stites, Randy, 67
Stites, Wilbur, 11
Stites, William, 73
Storm, Mr., 88
Stover, Mr., 85
Stover, Myron, 86, 87
Sutherland, Mr., 79, 81
Swartout, A. J., 43, 45

Taylor, Caroline, 45, 115
Taylor, Daniel, 43, 45, 115
Thomas, Warren, 117
Toirrents, John, 33
Towers, Richard, 88
Trueax, Mr., 45
Truman, Charles, 11, 42

Vansickle, Dr., 57
Vert, Louis, 73
Vinton, David, Jr., 43, 44, 63, 64
Vinton, David, Sr., 12, 13, 19, 43, 44
Vinton, Emma Harrison, 44, 63
Vinton, Frank H., 43, 44, 63, 64, 79
Vinton, Medad, 44
Vinton, Nellie, 49
Vinton, Sim, 45
Vinton, Will M., 43, 44
Voglie, John, 127

Wadsworth, Abram L., 105
Waggoner, Doris, 106
Waggoner, Ralph, 106
Warner, John, 89, 117, 127

Warner, Lucille Copeland, 82
Warner, Rose, 117, 127
Warner, William, 82
Watson Miriam, 80
Watson, Ada, 30, 48, 134
Watson, Annie Hamilton, 44, 47, 115
Watson, Barbara Ann, 118
Watson, Belle, 47
Watson, Ben, 47
Watson, Ben Adrian, 116, 118
Watson, Charlotte, 48
Watson, Claude, 47, 116
Watson, Claude Meacham, 118
Watson, Dorothy, 32, 47, 48
Watson, Fielding Benny, 3, 37, 41, 44, 47, 48, 80, 111, 113, 116
Watson, George, 16, 47
Watson, Gervas, Jr., 32, 41, 44, 47, 80, 111, 113, 115, 116, 131, 132
Watson, Gervas, Sr., 41, 44, 47, 79, 81, 113
Watson, Hammond, 47, 48
Watson, Helen, 48
Watson, Helen Pray, 30, 47
Watson, Hortense, 48
Watson, Hortense Kocher, 47
Watson, James, 25, 30, 47, 48
Watson, John, 30, 48, 80, 134
Watson, Kenneth, 68, 73, 134
Watson, Mabelle Corey, 47, 116, 118
Watson, Margaret, 48
Watson, Margaret Thompson, 32, 47, 116
Watson, Maude Gibbs, 47, 116
Watson, Sarah, 37, 44, 47, 53, 81
Watson, Sarah Lamson, 44, 47, 48, 116
Watson, Walter, 31, 32, 47, 48, 116, 135
Watson, William, 41, 44, 47, 80, 81, 113
Wedger, Mr., 123
Whistson, Helen, 138
White, John, Dr., 43, 45, 57, 63

White, Mr., 83
White, Ralph, 57, 63, 67
White, Ralph , 66
Whiting, Howard, 24
Wilhelm, Clarence, 116
Wilhelm, Mr., 24
Wilkes, Mr., 45, 83
Wilkinson, Wayne, 68
Williams, C. C., 9
Wills, Charles, 63, 66
Wills, Hugh, 63
Wills, Hugo, 63, 67
Withers, Mr., 45, 83
Wolf, Mr., 124
Wood, Amos, 141
Wood, Enoch, 141
Worden, Adolphus, 43
Worden, Agnes, 115, 118
Worden, Bertie, 50
Worden, Hattie, 82, 115
Worden, Loren, 50, 82, 115
Worden, Lulla, 50
Worden, Mattie, 50
Worden, Olive, 118, 137
Worden, Ralph, 50, 68, 115, 118
Worden, Sarah J., 45, 50, 115
Worden, Vern, 45, 115
Worden, Westen A., 45, 115
Worden, Weston A., 50
Worden,, Hattie Moshier, 139

Young, Almond, 37, 43, 44, 50, 82
Young, Alvie, 50, 82
Young, Bert, 50, 82
Young, Dora, 50, 82
Young, Emily, 44, 50, 82